Med
Hol, ...

SEARCHING FOR THE
BEYOND WITHIN

Sheldon B. Stephenson

PAULIST PRESS
New York/Mahwah, N.J.

Library of Congress Cataloging-in-Publication Data

Stephenson, Sheldon B.,   1920–
    Meditations on the Holy Spirit of God : searching for the beyond within / Sheldon B. Stephenson.
        p.   cm.
    ISBN 0–8091–3833–6 (alk. paper)
    1. Holy Spirit—Meditations. I. Title.
BT121.2.S825   1998
231'.3—dc21   98–39730
                                                                                                               CIP

Cover design: James F. Brisson
Interior design: Joseph E. Petta

Published by Paulist Press
997 Macarthur Boulevard
Mahwah, New Jersey 07430

www.paulistpress.com

Printed and bound in the
United States of America

CONTENTS

A Word of Appreciation

Even in the creative of moments no one works alone. Remembering the enjoyed moments of putting on paper what I believe to be Spirit-filled meditations, I want to express my gratitude to some special people:

My wife and friend, Charlotte, who was always there with joyful encouragement, even during some of my long periods of quietness.

Bishop Joseph H. Yeakel, my ecclesiastical leader and friend, for making sincere and constructive comments.

Lawrence Glazier, teacher of English and Shakespeare, who read the total manuscript and caringly shared thoughts about sentence structure and punctuation.

Alan M. Fletcher, internationally known and widely experienced editor of science journals, who made helpful stylistic and organizational suggestions.

FOREWORD

When we first met, Sheldon Stephenson, known by most as "Steve," was the pastor of the St. Paul's United Methodist Church in Ithaca, New York. Ithaca is the home of Cornell University and Ithaca College, where faculty and students permeate the life of the church as well as the whole city. Steve was a good and faithful pastor—a fine preacher—a confidant to students and faculty alike and open to the community of town and gown. He had been at this appointment for more than a decade. He had served as the chairman of the Tompkins County Social Planning Council and was a member of the city commission to rework the laws and ordinances for the city. He had led a group of people to the Soviet Union during the cold war and preached in missions in both Costa Rica and Nicaragua. He is a graduate with honors from the New York State College of Forestry and Boston University School of Theology. While in seminary he spent six months working with missionaries in Mexico.

United Methodist pastors are appointed to their churches, not called by the congregation. They are examined concerning their gifts, evidences of God's grace in their lives and the fruit of their efforts prior to their ordination. As Steve's bishop for twelve years, I "sent" him twice to his places of service.

His first appointment, following twelve years at St. Paul's Church, was the office of district superintendent. With his leadership, experience and ability to administer a large number of churches (eighty-five) while being a role model and mentor to incoming pastors, Steve proved his worthiness in this office.

One of the churches of his district was led by a brother pastor who felt called "by the Spirit" to leave our fellowship and to start an independent congregation, loyal to himself, right across the street from the church he had formerly served. This meant, also, taking along a substantial part of the congregation.

During these difficult and conflicting days Steve, as district superintendent, was a strong and stabilizing leader. At the annual conference it was my responsibility to appoint a pastor to the church so recently traumatized by division. Steve was the person, in my judgment, after prayer and consultation to pastor these people.

In that setting he grew in his experience and understanding of what he refers to in these meditations as "the Beyond Within"—that is, the work and meaning of the Holy Spirit in the lives of individual Christians and in the life of the church. Looking back over his life, he would tell you that the Spirit's presence working in and through him was a constant. This setting, however, with its ministry and focus, sharpened and shaped his understanding in new and, certainly, life-changing ways.

The devotions that follow are his reflections and convictions born in and growing out of his ordained-ministry journey over a half a century. We are invited to share the possibilities of our own spiritual formation as we read, meditate and pray under the guidance of Scripture and personal reflections of life's meaning and purpose for us.

Easter to Pentecost would be a most appropriate time to participate in these devotions; but, with the Holy Spirit, any time is really appropriate. These are written to and for believers, to help us experience "the Beyond Within"—and to live and serve faithfully as the Holy Spirit leads.

May it be so!

Bishop Joseph H. Yeakel
The United Methodist Church
November 1997

"I baptize you with water for repentance, but...
he will baptize you with the Holy Spirit and
with fire."

(Mt 3:11)

INTRODUCTION

When Jesus of Nazareth closed the door of the carpenter shop and that chapter of his life, he walked about seventy miles down along the Jordan River to the place where John the Baptizer was calling people to repentance and baptizing them with water as a sign of their new commitment to the way of God for their lives. When John saw Jesus coming he said to the people: "I baptize you with water, but...he will baptize you with the Holy Spirit and with fire" (Mt 3:11). When Jesus arrived, he asked John to baptize him.

As Jesus came up out of the water, his life was filled with the Holy Spirit of God; he heard God saying, "This is my beloved Son, with whom I am well pleased" (Mt 3:17). Isn't this the truth for us? Our experience of the Holy Spirit brings the realization of our relationship to God. We have read Romans 8:14: "[A]ll who are led by the Spirit of God are children of God."

Jesus came to baptize us with the Holy Spirit and with "fire." Most Christian creeds declare, "I believe in the Holy Spirit," but few say much about what that means to those who believe. Jesus came to bring to each of us a new life, full and abundant, a life that is morally and spiritually strong and vital, beauty-full and wonder-full. Jesus says to us, *"GOD IS SPIRIT!"* Jesus came inviting us to believe in him that we might know a deep and life-changing inner experience of this God who comes to us as Holy Spirit.

The Bible tells us that by the grace of God we are reconciled to God through our faith in Jesus the Christ. "[T]he Lord is the Spirit, and where the Spirit of the Lord is, there is freedom" (2 Cor 3:17). If the grace of God, the Holy Spirit of God, through our faith in Jesus Emmanuel ("God with us"), sets us free from our old selves to be reborn in the Spirit who is God, what really happens to us? What change does being born anew in the Spirit of God bring about within?

"God is Spirit." How does the Spirit-God relate to our inner lives? God comes to us as Creator, the Giver of life; God comes to us in Jesus the crucified and risen Lord; and God comes to our inner lives as Holy Spirit, bringing eternal meaning and purpose.

"God is love!" (1 Jn 4:8, 16) We experience this truth by the sacrificial love with which other people sometimes care for us; by the Christ whose life and death and resurrection reveal to us the sacrificial love and vitality of God within a human life; and by the willingness and the drive within our own spirits to pay the cost of loving others, even the "others" who may hurt us or be unwilling to accept our love.

We believe that the Holy Spirit presence in Jesus is the same Holy Spirit we experience. We remember Paul said, "[I]t is no longer I who live, but Christ who lives in me..." (Gal 2:20). God is love, but not just any kind of caring; God is sacrificial agape love. "Love is patient and kind; love is not jealous or boastful; it is not arrogant or rude. Love does not insist on its own way; it is not irritable or resentful; it does not rejoice at wrong, but rejoices in the right. Love bears all things, believes all things, hopes all things, endures all things. Love never ends..." (1 Cor 13: 4–8a). When you and I find ourselves loving with agape love, it is not we who love, but the Holy Spirit of God who is loving in and through us. If we trust, the Holy Spirit presence offers to us an ability to love far beyond our greatest expectations.

The Holy Spirit of God provides believers with special gifts for ministry. These gifts do not mean that we have any special holiness or that we are, in any way, better than others. It does mean that we are in a special way, "the salt of the earth," "the light of the world." It does mean that God is counting on us to use our gifts for the "common good." It does mean that our human purpose in life is "to glorify God and to enjoy him forever." It does mean that we are to bear witness to the God who is Holy Spirit. In a deep way, God's Spirit seems absent to the world. As people of God, our task is to bring to the lonely world the "Shekinah," the light and glory of the holy presence of God in our midst.

People who experience the Holy Spirit have a special "fire" and energy that "mere churchgoers" do not know. In our inner lives when we wait upon the Lord, we renew our strength; we mount up on wings like eagles; we run and are not weary; we walk and do not faint (see Is 40:31). J. B. Phillips, in his translator's preface to his paraphrase of the Acts of the Apostles, says this book of the Bible should be called, "The Acts of the Holy Spirit." Phillips declares that these people "did not make acts of faith, they believed; they did not say their prayers, they really prayed; they did not hold conferences on psychosomatic medicine, they simply healed the sick. Surely there was Someone here at work besides mere human beings. Consequently, it is a matter of sober historical fact that never before, or since, has any small group of ordinary people so moved the world that even their enemies with tears of rage in their eyes would say, 'These people have turned the world upside down!'" (Acts 17:6). Can the Christian church today survive without a powerful movement of the Holy Spirit within the lives of its people?

Experiencing the Holy Spirit is an exciting and joyous process. There is always something completely new and unexpectedly different. It is like coming into the presence of a huge light where you can see the beauty and meaning of a caring life more clearly than ever before. It may provide a new relationship to your family, friends and even enemies—give you a new perspective of your place in the struggle between good and evil—lead you deeper in your prayer time—show you new ways for using God's gifts to you—provide a greater vision of life's possibilities in Christ—give you a joy and a peace beyond your understanding.

Those who "faith" Christ, and allow the Holy Spirit to direct and drive their lives find themselves spiritually enriched. They experience within their souls "love, joy, peace, patience, kindness, goodness, faithfulness, gentleness, self-control" (Gal 5:22, 23a). These are Spirit qualities that those without the Holy Spirit cannot provide for themselves. As you meditate on this "fruit" of the Holy Spirit within, can you think of anything in all of life that you might want more? Is there anything that the lives of our children need more? Is there anything greater that God would dream for our lives? We are not to be immoral or ill-spirited people, because to do so is to sin against the Holy Spirit who wills to dwell in us.

A benediction in a worship service is not something we say to God, but, rather, something we prayerfully say to each other. In a benediction we often say, "May the grace of the Lord Jesus Christ, the love of God, the fellowship of the Holy Spirit be within each of us and all of us together, both now and always." It is my conviction that these blessings are all the same. The grace of the Lord Jesus Christ is the Love of God, is fellowship with the Holy Spirit. For me, the greatest joy possible is to experience this "Beyond Within."

At the inception of the long-lasting Roman Empire, Julius Caesar is quoted as saying, "I came; I saw; I conquered." At the inception of the forever-kingdom of God, Jesus came to baptize us with the Holy Spirit and with fire. So, you and I come; we read Scripture; we pray; and we entrust our forever-spirits to the life-vitality and guidance of the Holy Spirit of God.

SEARCHING FOR THE BEYOND WITHIN

Psalm 8   1 Corinthians 3:16–17   Psalm 23

It has been recited many times: "God is in his heaven and all is well in the world." Some of us spend our lives searching within our souls for the God beyond us out there in heaven.

When God seems distant we spend much of our time and energy trying to find certainties other than God to fill our emotional and spiritual needs. Older people do it in their old ways; younger people do it in newer but just as distracting ways. These days there are people who feel they can find all they need to know from a computer or on the Internet.

Sometimes we think about God as the great Creator who flings out the stars and the planets and creates a universe. We try to picture God as a power which can be formulated like $E=MC^2$—a gigantic and, perhaps ultimate, impersonal power.

Children often say, "May the force be with you!" The

Psalmist declares "O Lord, our Lord, how majestic is thy name in all the earth!...When I consider the work of thy fingers, the moon and the stars which thou has ordained, I ask, "What is man that thou art mindful of him?...Yet thou has made him a little less than God and crowned him with glory and honor."

In my deeper moments I realize that the Bible is not meaningful to me personally until it becomes "my Bible." I do not know Jesus as the Savior of the world until he becomes "my Savior." God is not truly a personal God until he becomes "my God." I cannot believe in eternal life until the Lord becomes "my shepherd." In our deeper spiritual yearnings we long to know, we search within our souls, for the Beyond God we have sensed "out there."

As we begin our heartfelt search we discover what we call the "grace" of God—we come to realize something we were not previously awake to—that the God we long to know within is reaching out to us. When our spirits need to be "born again," it is God's love for us personally in Jesus Christ that brings to us our needed change. "...not that we loved God but that he loved us" (1 Jn 4:10). When we see Jesus hanging on the cross because of the sins of the world, we come to believe it is for us individually and our sins that he died—that we might be redeemed.

We go to church and religious education classes and find others who also long to know God within. What joy and elation we find in fellowship with those like ourselves as we worship in spirit and in truth. The Scripture reading, the prayers, the singing of the hymns set us on fire to share with others this God within we are beginning to know.

This is only the beginning, because the God alive within

calls us to become "temples" in which his Holy Spirit may dwell. The Spirit moves us deeply in ever greater longings to know God within our souls. This spiritual motivation is not our doing. It is the grace of God calling out from within us to go on to the "perfection" of allowing the inner sanctifying presence of God to have his way with us.

This God within leads us to have an ever-increasing love for God and empowers us to have ever greater love for our family, our neighbors, and even our enemies. We gain "spiritual gifts to serve the common good" and fruits of the Spirit we have never known before. We long to share our experience of God with all around us. Our souls sing and shout praises for "our God," whom we know within.

PRAYER

Spirit of God descend upon my heart; wean it from earth, through all its pulses move; stoop to my weakness mighty as thou art and help me to love thee as I ought to love.
Hast thou not bid me love thee God and King, all, all thine own, soul, heart and strength, and mind? I see thy cross—there teach my heart to cling. O let me seek thee, and O let me find!
Teach me to love thee as thine angels love, one holy passion filling all my frame; the baptism of the heaven-descended dove; my heart an altar and thy love the flame. Amen.

—George Croly

IN THE BEGINNING—THE SPIRIT OF GOD

Genesis 1:1–5, 24–31

When a woman goes to the hospital and delivers a new-born life into the world, it is the most wonderful miracle possible. From whence does this life-full child receive its life, a selfhood all its own? Life is the most precious of all God's gifts.

We all wonder beyond our ability to wonder how life comes into being. Our Scripture tells us that in the beginning, when everything was void and without form, the Spirit of God moved on the face of the waters.

In humble worship we kneel in awe of God, because the Spirit-God is the One who began to create, and who, somehow, included us as part of his creation. God said, "Let there be light" (Gn 1:3) and there was light. God breathed into the dust of the earth and said, "Let us make man in our image, after our likeness"; and life began for us humans in God's creation. It seems that when God speaks, something that never before existed comes into being.

When everything was void and without form and dark, the Spirit of God moved on the face of the waters. It seems that God cares about order. When God speaks, a universe is created. Life comes into being that reproduces life, but only after its own kind. A day is defined because there is order: the day spoken of here begins with darkness covering the face of the earth; and then light comes into being. Darkness and light together, in that order, make one day; God thought that was good. Every atom, every molecule, every snowflake, every spider web has its order. We human beings praise God because he included us within his infinite and orderly universe.

When a child is born it begins its journey from birth to death. Its early, often wizened condition, reminds us of old age and its deteriorating physical life. We sometimes fear, we often wonder, does the creating Spirit care enough to bring this fragile earth-child to eternal life? Is this creating God able to give life eternal?

The Bible says, "Hear, O Israel: The Lord our God is one Lord" (Dt 6:4). The creating Spirit-God is the One, and the only one, who can make beauty and sense out of our lives, and, at the same time, powerful enough to open the door to eternal life for us.

PRAYER

Dear Holy Spirit, Creator-God, you are the Lord of Life. We confess that we find our meaning, our own oneness and its order, in your oneness. We are awed at your creating and life-giving power and grateful beyond measure to you for including us as part of life itself. We wonder what you want of us. Help us to worship you that your Spirit may permeate our being and make us yours. Ours is a broken and fragmented humanity. O Lord, help us to become whole and one in your oneness. We pray in all humility before you, our creating, Spirit-God. Amen.

SCRIPTURE AND THE HOLY SPIRIT

John 1:1–5; 9–14   Matthew 17:1–8
1 Corinthians 2:9–13

In my own prayer life I have found that my deeper spiritual experiences come as I read the Scriptures and, then, write out the prayer that follows. I am genuinely moved by spiritual insights I never could have had except for the Holy Spirit of God moving in my heart and mind, as I read the Scripture and write a prayer.

There is in Scripture reading a mysterious dynamic that moves us to ever deeper levels in our relationship to the God of Jesus. Reading Scripture is not just for the sake of information, but for insight; not just to learn something, but to experience God. As we read, the Holy Spirit becomes alive and present within us. Paul says to us: "Take...the sword of the Spirit, which is the word of God" (Eph 6:17).

We read about the Word or Logos, the expression of God, in the life of Jesus. "The Word became flesh and dwelt among us, full of grace [the Holy Spirit] and truth" (Jn 1:14). As I read this Scripture, my spirit reaches out toward Jesus. I begin to pray with expectation and excitement, trusting that this Holy Spirit will flood my being and become something of God's grace and truth within me. Believing in the incarnation of God in Jesus, I long to be a vital witness for the Spirit of God present in my own human life.

When I read the story of Jesus' transfiguration, envisioning the radiant countenance of Jesus, I hear God say about Jesus, "This is my beloved Son,...listen to him" (Mt 17:5). I read this again and again. As we meditate on the Gospels, they reveal Jesus as the Word of God to us. I believe the followers of Jesus longed to be transfigured, as Jesus was. I, too, pray to be. When I pray, I come to trust the redeeming power of the Christ and open my heart and mind, believing that if I am receptive enough, my whole physical countenance will shine and my spirit will come alive with the Holy Spirit of God. Some folks respond to this naturally with music, dance or art. I write a prayer.

The Bible is the Word of God to us. When Moses came down from the mountain with the Torah, the Law of God, written on stone tablets to show to the people, his face shone like the sun. They knew he had been with God, and they were afraid to come near. When a leader of worship speaks about the Scripture reading to the congregation, he or she often says: "This is the Word of God for all the people of God." Everyone responds, "Thanks be to God." There are still those who sit in back pews as though they were afraid to come too close to a word that God might speak to them. I believe the Bible is for all people who will read it and pray. Our faces will shine.

Our Scripture meditation tells us that as no one knows the thoughts of another person except that person, so no one can really know the thoughts of God except by the Spirit of God. If Scripture is God's way of leading us to the full, abundant life, how important is the Holy Spirit to those who long to understand the Word of God and to live with God and loved ones eternally?

The Holy Scriptures come alive for us when we realize that they share with us a God who was active millennia ago, but who is just as alive and available to us today in the person of the Holy Spirit.

PRAYER

Dear Spirit-God, we come to you humbly, so far from being the creatures you intend us to be. We thank you for the Bible, your holy Word to us. We become thought-filled and excited as your Holy Spirit becomes alive within us. Holy Spirit-God, touch our spirits and bless us, as we praise you in our precious moments of devotion. Amen.

THE SPIRIT-GOD WHO IS LOVE

Genesis 1:1–5   1 John 4:7–13

The most difficult thought for a human being is to try to picture what the infinite God is like. It seems impossible even to think about the One who has no beginning and no end, who is infinite in creativity and perfect in love.

When God was confronting Moses, sending him down to speak to the Pharaoh and to begin the Exodus of the Hebrew people, Moses asks of God, "Whom shall I say sent me?" God replies, "I am who I am; just tell them the 'I am' sent you" (Ex 3:14). How do we relate to the God who has no name, who just is?

What does this holy and eternal One have to do with this world—or with me? What does this purposeful God expect of me and mine? How do I relate to this Creator, Spirit-God, who loves me, and who brought me and mine and thee and thine into being?

Our Scripture tells us that God is love, agape love. God is not just any kind of love: God is sacrificial love. If you want to know what God is like, just kneel before the cross and look up into the face of the Savior of the world, sacrificing his life that we may be delivered from our sin, reconciled to the One who brought us into life. This is the Love-God redeeming the world. It is life-changing to realize that the infinite, Creator-God empathizes with his dust children in their suffering and death. The fruit of God's Spirit-presence is "Love..." (Gal 5:22).

God's love is the source of our ability to love one another. It is not that we first loved God, but that God loved us and sent Jesus to be the expiation for our unlovingness. If you experience some kind of total-being love for God, and if you can love others without counting the cost, you have something of God and agape love within you. This love-nature of God is revealed to us in Jesus who chose to be crucified on our behalf.

Albert Schweitzer once said, "The will to create and the will to love are the same." Can we understand anything about our Creator except as we experience agape love? No one has ever seen God; if we love one another as God in Christ has loved us, the Spirit-God abides in us (1 Jn 4:12).

PRAYER

Dear Spirit-God, we are deeply grateful that you are agape love, that we come to know you through the cross of Christ and through loving one another sacrificially. We confess, O God, in our lesser moments when we excuse our unloving behavior, we become self-centered, greedy, hateful and separated from you. We are made in your image and never meant to be mean or unkind.

Forgive us. We bow before you to pray that we, and others through us, may come to know you whose Holy Spirit is Love. Amen.

REMEMBERING HOLY SPIRIT EXPERIENCES

Nehemiah 9:18–23, 30–31
Psalm 139:7–18, 23–24

Some of my keenest experiences of the Holy Spirit have come in the remembrances of past moments when I had received some special blessing or arrived unexpectedly at an exciting place. Looking back at past events I realize that the Holy Spirit of God had been "prevenient grace" guiding me, touching me, without my knowing it.

Different people have asked me how I made the transition from the College of Forestry, with the all-absorbing science training there, to seminary. They think of this decision on my part and the change made as strange. Seminary was something I had never dreamed about, but it began for me the most life-changing and rewarding years I have known. I know now that it could never have happened without the Holy Spirit opening the way, leading me by the hand, and being present as just quiet, but exciting, inspiration.

Psalm 139 tells us that it is impossible to be where the Spirit of the Lord is not. The psalmist declares, "Thou didst knit me together in my mother's womb....Thy eyes beheld my unformed substance; in thy book were written, every one of them, the days that were formed for me, when as yet there were none of them" (Ps 139:13, 16).

When the Israelites returned from the Exile it was a benchmark in their history. Ezra and Nehemiah returned eager to rebuild the Holy City, Jerusalem; they longed to restore the Temple and the city walls. But the people were tired and hopeless about the possibilities. Ezra prays—he recalls the wilderness times of their people and how they rebelled against God, even making a golden calf to worship. He remembers that in those days God provided his "good Spirit" to instruct them. Even when they were evil, God, by his Spirit, warned them again and again. So, because of the Holy Spirit experiences of their ancestors, the people of Ezra and Nehemiah's day came to trust the Spirit of God to be adequate in leading them in their restoration of the Holy City. This remembrance enabled the people to do that which, in their frail humanity, they never could have dreamed possible. The Spirit of God had inspired their ancestors and, in this remembrance, they went forward to rebuild.

Worship is essential to our spiritual lives. In worship we rehearse the mighty acts of God in the history of our people and in our own past. When we come to experience the Lord's Supper we remember that night when Jesus and his disciples shared the broken bread and poured out wine. We remember that Jesus said, "This is my body which is broken for you. This cup is a new covenant in my blood." We do what we do "in remembrance." Now when we gather for the Lord's Supper, it becomes for us a sacrament and we realize ourselves being spirit-fed as the disciples were so long ago. When we remember the Lord Jesus and worship in Spirit we are born anew.

The Holy Spirit is continually striving to touch our lives and to lead us on. Many times we do not recognize this presence until later when we recall how previously we had been blessed. It is life-changing to remember prior Holy Spirit experiences.

PRAYER

Dear Lord God, Holy Spirit, you are constantly trying to bless us and lead us; we are too busy or too callous to pay attention, or to be thankful. Forgive us, O Lord, for our preoccupations, our lack of faith or outright sin, blocking a deep spirit-filled life with you. All through history, O God, you have led people out of captivity, through difficult seas, to the promised land. Help us to worship you deeply in spirit and in truth, to fast, and to pray, that never again shall we miss the daily opportunities of our lifetime to know your grace, your love, your Holy Spirit present with us. Amen.

THE SPIRIT WHO CALLS AND WHO ANOINTS

Isaiah 61:1–3   Psalm 23   James 5:13–15

Have you ever felt that the Spirit of God was touching your life, and, perhaps, inviting you to carry out a particular purpose? What do you think God wants with your life? In the Bible God calls people from all walks of life to live for many different reasons: Deborah, Jonah, Isaiah, Hannah, Mary, Matthew, Saul....

It was an opportunity of my life as a teenager to work one summer, away from everyone I knew, in a lumber camp. All of the people there spoke languages foreign to me, and I was lonely. This gave me the opportunity to spend some time alone with my Bible. In those quiet moments my life was changed; I felt a real call to come out of myself and become a pastor to people who might be lonely. I had a hard time believing, and I had all sorts of reasons for not responding.

God is Spirit who touches our lives and calls us to be something special for him. Do we not need to take enough time to allow God to tell us, or show us, what that might be?

One of my favorite Scriptures is Isaiah 6:1–8. As the young Isaiah is worshiping in the temple, confessing his sin, the voice of God asks: "Whom shall I send, and who will go for us?" (v. 8). This youth hears himself crying out, "Here am I! Send me!" Isaiah could not know what would be ahead for him—that he would become the outstanding prophet of all of Israel; but he knew that God's Spirit was touching his life, anointing him to become something special for his people. Suppose there is something special and different for each of us?

Even Jesus, in the synagogue at Nazareth, would express the vision of his own mission: "The Spirit of the Lord is upon me, because he has anointed me to preach good news to the poor" (Lk 4:18). Read again Isaiah 61:1–3.

For many, being anointed with oil is a healing experience. The disciples of the Lord went out; "...they cast out many demons, and anointed with oil many that were sick and healed them" (Mk 6:13). I have had parishioners, needing to be forgiven and healed, ask me to anoint them with oil. James says: "Is any among you sick? Let...the elders pray over him, anointing him with oil in the name of the Lord" (5:14–15).

When one feels called by God and anointed by the Holy Spirit, life becomes extraordinarily beautiful and richly rewarding. "Our cups runneth over."

PRAYER

Dear anointing Lord, we recognize that you are Spirit. Without you we are nothing; but with you we have eternal meaning. As Jesus realized your Spirit was upon him, anointing him for your redeeming mission, so we pray your Holy Spirit will anoint our lives. We pray, longing to be healed and spirit-filled. Cleanse us, heal us, bless us, anoint us; in the name of Jesus, and for our own sakes, we pray. Amen.

HOLY SPIRIT-POTTER

Jeremiah 18:1–6   Psalm 2:7–9
2 Corinthians 5:17–21

Jeremiah holds before us the picture of God as our Potter, with us as the clay.

In the words of Adelaide A. Pollard, the hymn declares:

> Have thine own way, Lord; Have thine own way.
> Thou art the Potter, I am the clay.
> Mold me and make me after thy will,
> while I am waiting yielded and still.

The Lord God said to Jeremiah: "Arise, and go down to the potter's house, and there I will let you hear my words" (18:2). As Jeremiah watched the potter work, the vessel he was working on became marred and spoiled. But, like God, the potter took the spoiled clay and reworked it into a new and perfect vessel. The Lord declared, "Can I not do with you, as this potter has done [with this clay]?" (18:6).

Part of the image of the potter and the clay is that the

potter, himself, can destroy the imperfect vessel. We human vessels are judged by the Spirit of God, and our wrongly oriented lives can be broken by the same God who brought us into life. In Psalm 2, God seems to be speaking to the Messiah, saying: "I will make the nations your heritage,...and [you will] dash them to pieces like a potter's vessel." Indeed, if the Potter is to reshape our lives, do we not need to repent of our evil ways, and turn ourselves back to the Potter for reshaping into something spiritually beautiful and more useful? Indeed, it seems that the redeeming Spirit of God is constantly trying to reshape our spirits. We are to be born again in the Spirit. "[I]f any one is in Christ, he is a new creation; behold, the old has passed away, the new has come." Jesus the Christ becomes the pattern for our reshaping. In Christ's pattern we are to love one another as Christ has loved us; we are to forgive each other as God in Christ has forgiven us; we are to go on toward the perfection we see in Christ.

Jesus came to baptize us with the Holy Spirit. The Holy Spirit is God's presence in us, the Spirit-Power, shaping and reshaping our spirit lives. The Holy Spirit presence gives us a certitude that we are forgiven. He heals our brokenness and empowers us to grow in grace according to the pattern of Christ. In the Holy Spirit, we are given re-created lives to live for the glory of Christ.

PRAYER

Dear Lord, Holy Spirit-Potter, we are deeply sorry for our sins, for the evils of society in which we have participated; but even more, for those times when we failed to become the persons of the spiritual depth and beauty you have intended us to be. Break us, if you must. We ask for your forgive-

ness and your grace. We pray that you may be our Potter and take us to be the clay. Work on us, fashion and refashion us, until we become spirit-filled; anxious to become more and more like Jesus the Christ, our Lord. Amen.

CREATE IN ME A CLEAN HEART, O GOD

Psalm 51:7–17

We are told, actually commanded, to love the Lord our God with all our heart...(See Dt 6:5). Many of us would like to be able to do just that. We would like to have a singleness of heart and mind about God. But our hearts, our souls, are often divided in their loyalties and their loves. We may be tired trying to love everybody. We may not even be sure what our "hearts" really are.

The heart is the intellectual center, but it is greater than just our thinking; it also controls how we feel. The heart is the driving force of our total being and chooses the direction and the commitment with which we journey. The heart is the "spirit" in which we live; the heart is who we really are. "Cleanness" is the presence of God's Spirit and a purity of heart in our love for God.

We run amuck when our hearts are profane or immoral, conceited or violent. When these things are the substance of our being, our whole lives are totally warped out of shape, alienating us from our God. In Mark 1 we read how evil spirits convulsed human lives, making people sick and distraught. Jesus began his ministry driving out these evil spirits, enabling people to become healthy in body and soul. We need to become clean, and only God can do that for us. Our Scripture says: "Purge me with hyssop, and I shall be clean; wash me, and I shall be whiter than snow" (Ps 51:7).

The psalmist knew what we know and felt what we feel. He longed for the salvation of his soul. He would teach transgressors the ways of God. He prayed that God might deliver him from bloodguiltiness (murder of someone not deserving it). He wanted to praise God. He would tell all about the salvation the Lord God had given him. He realized that only God could save him from himself. He would declare that the only sacrifice acceptable to God was a broken and a contrite heart.

The psalmist understood the "presence" to be the Holy Spirit of God. It was the Holy Spirit alone who could give him a clean heart and his only hope. He prayed that the Lord would not take the Holy Spirit away from him.

PRAYER

Create in me a clean heart, O God, and put a new
and right spirit within me.
Cast me not away from thy presence, and take not
thy holy Spirit from me.
Restore to me the joy of thy salvation, and uphold
me with a willing spirit.

Deliver me from bloodguiltiness..., and my tongue
will sing aloud of thy deliverance.

O Lord, open thou my lips, and my mouth shall
show forth thy praise....

The sacrifice acceptable to God is a broken spirit; a broken and contrite heart, O God, thou wilt not despise.

Create in me a clean heart, O God, and put a new and right spirit within me (Ps 51:10–12, 14–17). Amen.

NOT BY MIGHT NOR BY POWER,
BUT BY SPIRIT, SAYS THE LORD

Zechariah 4:6–9

What brings power to a human life? What gives us true vitality in our living?

As human beings we seem to glory in what we perceive to be our power. Nations want political and military might so they may not be afraid of their foes. In our families husbands and wives sometimes vie with each other about who makes the decisions, who controls the money, who has his or her wishes met first.

Power is a strange thing. There is a difference between that which seems most powerful and what is right or wrong. A political person may exhibit great leadership abilities, but be, at the same time, a tyrant. A husband or a wife may control the finances of a family and even be good at it, but still be mean or selfish. Some folks are able to begin a very important work, but lack the power to finish.

The power needed for human living is different and special. An ax may work for splitting a log, but it probably will not help to heal a broken family relationship. A gun may keep an enemy at bay, but it does not improve the wisdom or the goodness of the person who holds the gun.

The words of our Scripture are directed to a man by the name of Zerubbabel, a leader in the return of the Hebrew exiles to Jerusalem. People looked to him with expectation because he was a governor and because he was of the lineage of David. Somehow he participated in the rebuilding of the Temple. He epitomized the dream that one day the Davidic line would once more be the ruling power in Israel. How could he help bring to reality this great dream?

"This is the word of the Lord to Zerubbabel: 'Not by might, nor by power, but by my Spirit says the LORD of hosts'" (Zec 4:6).

The Spirit of the Lord heals wounds, mends broken friendships and empowers a human life with love and courage.

We are to worship the Lord our God in spirit and in truth, not just because we should worship, but also because it is through our worship, our praise of the Lord, that we find the Spirit of the Lord revitalizing us with a love of life, courage and stamina.

When Jesus teaches us to pray the most nearly perfect prayer, we conclude with the soul-lifting words to God, "For thine is the kingdom and the power and the glory forever."

Our purpose is to seek the kingdom of God: the power needed for our seeking is not our own, but the presence of the Holy Spirit of God. The kingdom and the power and the glory belong to the Spirit-God.

PRAYER

Offer to God our Lord's Prayer.

BORNE UP ON EAGLES' WINGS

Isaiah 40:28–31   Ephesians 3:14–19
Exodus 19:3–5

In one of Gilbert and Sullivan's operas, there is a line that asks what thieves do when they are not thieving. The response is they are sitting by the brook and smelling the flowers. Most people have good intentions and dreams for their lives. Some live out their vision of a good life, but many simply do not have the spiritual strength to follow through. Our Scripture says, "Even youths shall faint and be weary, and young [people] shall fall exhausted" (Is 40:30).

A minister was preaching outdoors to a group of home-less, defeated people. He quoted a line from Kipling: "If you can fill each hour with sixty seconds worth of dis-tance run..." From the back, an alcoholic's stammering voice cried out, "But what if you can't?" The truth is that most of us can't. We may envision a great life, but it is difficult, if not impossible, to live it out.

We believe that we are indeed saved by the grace of

God. What does the Holy Spirit of God do for a human life? Listen to Isaiah: "They who wait upon the Lord shall renew their strength, they shall mount up on wings like eagles; they shall run and not be weary; they shall walk and not faint!"

Paul, writing to the Ephesians, declares: "I bow my knees before the Father...that...you may be strengthened with might through his Spirit [in your inner life]...[that you may] know the love of Christ...[and] be filled with all the fullness of God." In writing to the Philippians, Paul put it this way: "I can do all things in him [Christ] who strengthens me" (4:13). Jesus came to enable us to know the life abundant. Will he not give us the spiritual strength to live out his dream for us?

> In her book, *The Helper,* Catherine Marshall says: "In our time we can observe two groups of Christians—those who have Christ with them, and those who have Christ in them. The second group knows the 'vine life' is the only one that is going to bring heaven's power to earth and secure results. Their life has to be inside the vine, an integral part of its very cells and its flow. This inside life is what the Spirit makes possible to us" (p. 34). Isn't the Spirit presence our real and lasting life vitality?

By myself I am lonely and afraid. No one can stand alone for very long. The Holy Spirit who kept Jesus strong and courageous is the same Spirit of God who dwells within us.

We recall the words of the hymn by Michael Joncas:

> And He will raise you up on eagle's wings,
> bear you on the breath of dawn,

make you to shine like the sun;
and hold you in the palm of his hand.

PRAYER

Dear Lord God, we come to you, confessing our weaknesses, yearning to live the dream of life you hold before us. Lord, we wait upon you; we pray that you will renew our moral and spiritual strength and bear us up on eagles' wings; that we may run and not be weary, that we may walk and not faint. Amen.

THE BIRTH OF JESUS

Matthew 1:18–25   Luke 1:26–35
John 1:14–18

In our Christian faith and in our human life we try to understand how Jesus was related to God. How did this child, Jesus, become the Christ Child?

We read that God so loved the world that he sent Jesus. At first it seemed that God had sent Jesus, as though God were the bow and Jesus was the arrow.

The disciples, in trying to understand Jesus' relationship to God, needed to have another concept. At first they thought God had sent Jesus, but then they said God came with Jesus. Even this was not good enough. Finally they said that God came in Jesus. The child Jesus sent by God was really "Emmanuel (which means, God with us)" (Mt 1:23). Our experience of God in Jesus makes Jesus the Christ for us.

The Holy Spirit is the creating aspect of God (Gn 1:1–2). In our faith the Holy Spirit visited a young maiden of

Nazareth and declared she would bear a child who would be the Son of God. Henceforth, all people would call her blessed (joyous). An angel would sing, "For to you is born this day...a Savior, who is Christ the Lord" (Lk 2:11). A star would shine over his manger. All his life Jesus would experience the presence of the Holy Spirit. He would understand that the Holy Spirit initiated his life and would bring to him the vision of his ministry. The Holy Spirit would provide the necessary resources and spiritual strength he needed.

In a deeper sense, the Spirit of God became the Spirit of Jesus, the Savior of the world. For us, Jesus is the Spirit-God manifesting himself to his world.

In the gospel of John we hear about the *logos* of God, the Word of God. *Logos* really means more than just "word"; as stated earlier, it means the expression of God. The Logos is God expressing himself in the universe. This expression of God became flesh and dwelt among us, full of grace and truth. This grace, this Spirit, came to us, alive, in Jesus of Nazareth. No one has ever seen God; this Holy Spirit-Child, this Word of God, has made God known to us (Jn 1:18).

PRAYER

Dear Spirit-God, we thank you for your gift to us, your Holy Spirit-Child. We know you are Spirit, indeed Holy Spirit. In Jesus we see your very Spirit present in life. We read about the star shining, and the angels singing—what a beautiful scene! We picture the shepherds and the magi coming and kneeling before this Holy Spirit-Child. And so we, too, come to kneel, to pray and to offer our lives. Touch us, O Lord God, as you touched

Mary's life, that your Spirit-Child may be born in us, filling our lives, enabling us to belong to you. With our faith in this Christ Child, we would offer our prayer. Amen.

HOLY SPIRIT-CHILD—EMMANUEL (GOD WITH US)

Matthew 1:18–25

What do you call this child born of Mary in Bethlehem? Do you suppose Mary and Joseph called him "son"? Probably they called him "Jesus," as the angel had instructed them. It was a common name at that time.

The Scriptures tell us that he was a Holy Spirit-Child, and, therefore, would be known as "Emmanuel" ("God with us").

Some people of Nazareth called him "the carpenter." Why not? He had worked at the household trade until he was about thirty years old. When Jesus was baptized, the Holy Spirit filled his life. God whispered, "This is my beloved child, my beloved son." We call him "the son of the living God."

The disciples called him "Rabbi," for he was their teacher. Once during a journey to Caesarea Philippi, Jesus asked the disciples who people thought he was. They responded, "Some people say John the Baptist, others say Elijah, and others Jeremiah or one of the prophets" (Mt 16:14). Then, Jesus asked them, "Who do you say that I am?" (Mt 16:15). Out of the blue Peter sputtered, "You are the Christ, the Son of the living God" (Mt 16:16). Actually, Peter did not use the word "Christ," the Greek word; Peter used "Messiah," meaning one who would deliver the kingdom from the Romans to Israel. But, for that moment, at least, they thought of Jesus as the Messiah, the One who builds the Church.

In the "Hallelujah Chorus" of Handel's *Messiah,* we sing, "He is King of kings; he is Lord of lords." In the carol by Tom Colvin, "That Boy-Child of Mary," the question is raised, "What shall we call him, child of the manger? What name is given in Bethlehem?" (© Hope Publishing Co.)

In our Scripture meditation, Mary was "with child of the Holy Spirit" (v. 18). Joseph was startled at this, but the angel reassured him; "Joseph, son of David, do not fear to take Mary for your wife, for that which is conceived in her is of the Holy Spirit" (Mt 1:20). I wager that the community of Nazareth was surprised when Joseph told them that the child of Mary was not really his, but the child of the Holy Spirit. I wonder if Joseph referred to Jesus as "Holy Spirit-Child."

Christmas means "The Christ Mass," the time we come to our churches and fall on our knees in worship before this one whom God has sent to redeem the world. This Christ Child is the Savior of the world.

What shall we call this gift of God to us? Let's all call him, "Emmanuel," "God with us." We could really celebrate!!

PRAYER

Dear God in Jesus, we thank you for coming to us. Without you we are lost and wander aimlessly. We sometimes work hard, but our work without you is meaningless. We need a Savior! You sent to us this Holy Spirit-Child. In him you grant us a vision of life with you. We would celebrate the "Christ Mass." We offer ourselves to this beautiful life-person, this Emmanuel, God with us. Amen.

THE SACRAMENT OF JESUS' BAPTISM

Luke 3:15–22

What happens to a person who comes to be baptized? In some churches this experience of being baptized is called a "sacrament." This means that the person experiences the grace of God, the Holy Spirit of God.

When John the Baptist baptized people, he called them first to repent their separations from God. People came in large numbers. Apparently the doorway to a new relationship with God opens as we express sorrow for the times when we have not had the spirit of God in our hearts. When we have hurt other people or have surrendered to the temptation to be someone less than that whom we believe God has in mind for us to be, we alienate ourselves from God.

What sort of God do we meet at our baptism? Is it not a God of grace, who, if our confession is sincere, offers us forgiveness and holds before us a life more loving, more beautiful, more rewarding, than any dream we might hold for ourselves?

After all the others had been baptized, Jesus, himself, came to be baptized. It is difficult to know what this meant to the perfect one. It seemed to him, and to everyone present, that the Holy Spirit had come into his life. Jesus could hear God saying of him, "This is my beloved Son, in whom I am well pleased." For me, there was something of this in my own baptism. I had a strange and wondering experience of being, in a new way, a child of God—a God of grace, who expects great things from me.

After his baptism, a new life began for Jesus. He had been a carpenter, working at the household trade. Now Jesus would go forth baptizing people with the Holy Spirit of God and with fire. Now Jesus would feel himself anointed for a special ministry, directed by the Holy Spirit. He would say, "The Spirit of the Lord is upon me, because he has anointed me to preach good news..." (Lk 4:4). Because Jesus participated in the event and received the Holy Spirit, we call baptism a sacrament. To be baptized is to receive God's grace—to participate in a sacrament. Friends of mine have traveled all the way to the Holy Land so they might experience in a special way the grace of God by being baptized in the Jordan River.

Have you in your meditation time ever allowed John the Baptist to speak to you, calling you to repent of your separation from the Lord who loved you into life? Have you ever, in your faith in Christ, been baptized and heard God say to you, "You are my beloved child in whom I am well pleased?" This is God's grace especially for you!—a true sacrament!

PRAYER

Dear Lord God, we have sinned against you and are not worthy to be called your children. You have called us to repent of our un-Christlike spirit and challenged us to follow the Lord Jesus into a new life of meaning and service. Baptize us afresh with your Holy Spirit. We worship you, our God; for to you belong all the glory and the praise. We are told that Jesus received your Holy Spirit when he prayed. We come to you in his name, O Lord, and we, too, pray. Amen.

JESUS' TEMPTATIONS

Luke 4:1–15   Hebrews 4:15, 16

Jesus taught us to pray to the God who loves us, "Lead us not into temptation, but deliver us from evil." He taught us to pray this, because it is God's kingdom that we need to enter; it is God's power that we need to overcome our temptations, and it is before God's glory that we are to bow each day.

The writer of Hebrews declares that we should draw near to the throne of grace, believing that we shall receive the grace and mercy we long for in our times of spiritual need. We can do this because our "high priest," Jesus, was tempted in every way, just as we are. Jesus, knowing our temptations, knows how we need the Spirit of God to overcome our weaknesses.

At Jesus' baptism the Holy Spirit flooded his life. For some reason, he was led by the Holy Spirit into the wilderness to confront the "tempter" and the subsequent temptations that were his. Indeed, Mark, in his gospel, says, "The Spirit immediately drove him [Jesus]

out into the wilderness" (Mk 1:12), as though Jesus himself were reluctant to go. This seems strange to us at
first, because we usually think of the Spirit of God taking away our temptations and delivering us from evil.

Jesus was confronted with the temptation to turn stones
into bread. Why not? The people were poor and hungry.
Why wouldn't it be a good idea to turn stones into
bread? The reason, we know, is that people need more
than bread alone. They need, we need every word that
proceeds from the mouth of God. Jesus would live his
life for a greater good.

The tempter took Jesus to the top of a high mountain
and showed him all the kingdoms of the world. He told
Jesus he could have all of these kingdoms if he would
just fall down and worship him. Why not? Jesus is Lord,
and he should have all the kingdoms of the world. Jesus
could not do this, because in life the means determine
the end. No one comes to any good by evil or ungodly
means—not in God's world. Jesus answered, "You shall
worship the Lord your God, and him only shall you
serve" (Lk 4:8).

Were not the temptations of Jesus similar to our own?
Are not our greatest temptations to give ourselves to
cheaper, unfulfilling ends and to serve lesser gods?

The Holy Spirit alone is powerful enough to lead us
beyond our temptations, to live lives worthy of our God.
We can have confidence in this because the presence of
the Holy Spirit enabled Jesus to overcome his temptations. We, too, can draw near the throne of grace to
receive mercy and grace in our time of need. The Holy
Spirit present with Jesus in his temptations is also present with us in ours.

PRAYER

Dear Lord God, fill us with your Holy Spirit that we may be spiritually vital and strong. In your mercy forgive us for the times when we have fallen before our temptations. Help us to know that your Holy Spirit is the only companion who can lead us beyond our littleness to the glory and beauty of the Christian life. We pray in the name of Jesus, our Lord and Savior, who was tempted in every way as we are, but who, in your Spirit, was truly victorious. Amen.

JESUS ANOINTED BY THE HOLY SPIRIT

Luke 4:14–21   Acts 10:34–38

After his temptations, Jesus returned from the wilderness to Nazareth, in the power of the Holy Spirit. On the Sabbath Day he went to the synagogue, as was his custom, and there he declared to the people the direction of his ministry by quoting from the prophet, Isaiah:

"The Spirit of the Lord is upon me because he has anointed me to preach the gospel to the poor, to heal the broken hearted, to proclaim release to the captives, and the recovery of sight to the blind, to set at liberty those who are oppressed, and to proclaim the acceptable year of the Lord (Lk 4:18, 19 KJV). The Spirit of God anointed Jesus to "seek and to save the least, the last, and the lost."

The word, "anoint," implies a commissioning, a leading of some kind from God. Kings, priests, prophets, sacred places—and Jesus—were anointed. Jesus' ministry began with his being anointed by the Spirit of God.

Peter tells the people about Jesus, beginning with his

baptism by John, and describes how "God anointed Jesus of Nazareth with the Holy Spirit and with power." Peter said, "[This Jesus] went about doing good and healing all who were oppressed...for God was with him" (Acts 10:38). Peter spoke these words to Cornelius, a Gentile, indicating that God's loving Spirit was for everyone, not just a chosen few. As we read the New Testament, we see clearly that the Holy Spirit had commissioned Jesus and led him throughout his ministry.

The presence of the Holy Spirit in Jesus' life gave authenticity and power in his ministry. Jesus of Nazareth, filled with the Holy Spirit of God, is the Savior of the world.

The Holy Spirit in Jesus becomes, at least, a living presence in whom God sets before us the essence of life itself. ("In him [Jesus] was life, and the life was the light of [people everywhere]" Jn 1:4.)

John the Baptist said that Jesus would baptize us with the Holy Spirit and with fire. Apparently Jesus, anointed by the Holy Spirit, had the mission to share this grace of God with us. "To all who received him, who believed in his name, he gave power to become children of God" (Jn 1:12). There is a deep truth in life that those who are led by the Spirit have a genuineness and a power, as they bear witness to the Spirit-God in their lives.

PRAYER

Dear Lord God in Jesus, we believe that your Holy Spirit presence in us is the very essence of life itself. Help us to accept and to believe in Jesus as your Messiah. We meditate on the meaning of Christ, and we believe in Christ's ability to baptize us with your Spirit. We believe that Jesus is the way and the truth and the life; no one truly comes to you except through him. Jesus, anointed by your Holy Spirit, is your Word, your Spirit-Child, your redeeming Messiah for the world. We praise you, Holy Spirit-God, for loving us enough to come to the world in Jesus the Christ. We pray in his name. Amen.

OUR CHRISTIAN FAITH AND THE HOLY SPIRIT

1 Corinthians 12:1–3   1 Corinthians 2:9–13

No one can say, "Jesus is Lord," except by the Spirit. Jesus came to baptize us with the Holy Spirit. It is our inner experience of God that gives us the certitude that Jesus is Lord.

Jesus teaches us to love God with all our heart and mind, soul and strength; and to love one another as he has loved us. Following these commandments, Jesus says, leads us to experience eternal life. Is it not the presence of the Holy Spirit that enables us to love at all; and, especially, to love one another with the agape love Jesus lived? Jesus taught us that only as we forgive are we forgiven. Why should we believe this? It is as we shed our self-centeredness, inviting Jesus to be the Christ of our lives, forgiving those who have hurt us, that we experience deeply the joy of the Holy Spirit and know for certain, that Jesus is Lord.

It is through our Holy Spirit experience that we are enabled to comprehend the thoughts of God. It is the

Spirit who helps us to appreciate something of the vast-ness of life God has in store for us. "What no eye has seen, nor ear heard,...what God has prepared for those who love him, God has revealed to us through the Spirit....[We are] taught by the Spirit, interpreting spiritual truths to those who possess the Spirit....The Spirit reveals every-thing, including the depths of God" (1 Cor 2:9–13).

As we experience the Holy Spirit loving in us and through us, we come to believe that loving is, for us and for all people, the full and abundant life. We come to believe that we, too, have a mission, a God-given pur-pose in which we are to live and find our eternal mean-ing. It is the presence of the Holy Spirit in our lives that enables us to believe in Christ; yes, to believe deeply in Christ as our Savior and Lord with our total being, and also to believe in ourselves and our own worth. It is the Holy Spirit presence that enables us to realize that God knows and loves us, each one, personally. Paul says that our Christian faith is "sealed" by the presence of God's Holy Spirit (Eph 1:13).

It is the Holy Spirit in each of us who unites us in a *koinonia* fellowship the world cannot know. In this fel-lowship we are able to worship together, in one Spirit, the living God who abides within us.

"Jesus is Lord!" He is the way and the truth and the life, but no one can say this confidently without the Holy Spirit.

PRAYER

O Holy Spirit-God, enable me to know for sure that "Jesus is Lord" and to declare this confidently to my family and neighbors. Help me to have faith in Jesus as the Christ; help me to believe in you as a living and loving God. Help me to believe in myself as your spirit-child who can live with the eternal purpose and mission of loving others as Christ has loved me. I believe; baptize me, O Holy Spirit, for Jesus' sake. Amen.

THE SPIRIT WHO IS TRUTH

John 8:31–32   John 14:15–17   John 15:26–27
John 18:37–38   2 Timothy 1:11–14

Jesus stood before Pilate, the one who had the decision as to whether Jesus would continue to live or to die. He asks Jesus, "So you are the King?" He wonders who Jesus really is. Jesus responds: "For this [reason] I was born, and for this [reason] I have come into the world, to bear witness to the truth." Pilate asks, "What is truth?" (Jn 18:37–38). Isn't this the question most of us ask? We want to know the truth of our identity and our life's meaning.

We tend to believe that real truth is hard to come by. For us, truth changes with the passing of time or with the changing of circumstances surrounding us. We seem to think that real truth is in an equation, or found on the Internet. We seem to have lost our sense of virtue, the eternal truth Jesus brings to us.

One Christmas Eve, about supper time, I was walking down the main street of our small town. It was snowing and everything seemed beautiful to me. I was looking forward to the Christmas Eve service at our church. I happened to see a friend of mine going into the liquor store. Knowing this was a problem with him, I stopped him and said, "Bill, you do not need to go in there; you need to go home." He stopped and, with a rather sad countenance, looked at me. He said, "Steve, you do not know how it is to go to my home." That was a truth; I did not know how it would be to go home to his home. But what was truth for him? Would he find the truth in the liquor store or in going to those difficult ones who waited for him at home? The truth for Bill will not come until he experiences the Holy Spirit dealing with his personal spiritual problems. What is the truth that Jesus declares "sets us free"?

Jesus says, "If you love me, you will keep my commandments. And I will pray the Father, and he will give you another Counselor,...even the Spirit of truth" (Jn 14:15–17). The word translated here, "Counselor," comes from a root word meaning, "someone who will stand with us and help us to be brave." The "Counselor" for Jesus was the Holy Spirit. When we obey Jesus, the Holy Spirit, who is truth, stands with us.

The Holy Spirit dwelling in us is our certitude of God's living reality. The Holy Spirit is the truth who, in our lives, helps us to stand up bravely, as a witness to God's presence.

God's Spirit is agape, sacrificial love, the greatest of all things that really last, the eternal truth. When you and I have some element of this sacrificial spirit for each other, together, we share the Spirit of truth.

PRAYER

O God, we thank you, for all those in whose lives your truth is seen. Remove from us any spirit that perverts your truth. Give us minds and hearts that can see at once the difference between the true and the false. Help us to test every spirit, and to hold fast to the Counselor. Grant us the grace to live the Spirit-Truth we know in Jesus Christ our Lord. Amen.

THE SPIRIT WHO FORGIVES

Matthew 5:43–48   Matthew 6:14–15
Acts 7:54–8:1a   Hebrews 10:15–17

If some one hurts you, it is a very difficult matter to forgive. If some one has committed a serious crime against another human being, it seems only right that the person should be isolated from the society.

If you have hurt someone, how do you ask to be forgiven? If your sin is immorality, spite, revenge, something contrary to the Spirit of God, how can you expect to be forgiven? How can you get beyond your sin?

In society there are those who insist that the only way to stop some evil people is the death penalty. They ask, "However do you bring justice to a family who has lost a child to a drunken driver or to someone who has sold 'crack' to their child?"

There are those who think of God as an avenging God. Are there sins for which God is unwilling to forgive? The Bible tells us that sin against the Holy Spirit is unforgivable. Will the God who is Holy Spirit hold always some things against us when the spirit of our lives is ungodly?—or unforgiving?

The Spirit of Christ is "grace." The cross of Jesus stands before us as an unconditional offer of forgiveness. This Spirit of Christ is not only a forgiving spirit, but also a spirit who redeems us from our own inability to forgive. This offer of redemption, like a coin, has two sides. It calls upon us to repent of our sin against others and, also, at the same time, to forgive the people who have sinned against us or hurt us. The Scripture tells us that unless we forgive, we are not really open to receive forgiveness ourselves.

It is the Holy Spirit within us who causes us, humbly, to ask for forgiveness and provides for us the willingness to forgive others.

Stephen, the first Christian martyr, forgiving those who were stoning him to death, personifies the Spirit who alone can redeem the world. As a consequence, Saul the persecutor, being touched by the Spirit of Jesus, became Paul, the great apostle of Christ.

Paul writing to the Colossians (3:14–15) says, "Put on love, which binds everything together....And let the peace of Christ rule in your hearts." It is the Holy Spirit at work within us who enables us to know the peace of forgiving ourselves. The Spirit is God's "grace," which alone can redeem our unforgiving lives.

Christ from the cross cries out, "Father, forgive them; for they know not what they do!" (Lk 23:34). The Spirit of Christ intercedes for us, praying that God will redeem us from the unforgiving evil that swamps us.

The forgiving Spirit of God breaks down the barriers

between us and those from whom we have been alien-
ated, healing our brokenness. It is the Spirit of forgiveness, dissolving hurts and suffering, touching both our
lives and the lives of those separated from us. We are
asked to forgive our enemies and to pray for those who
persecute us, so we may become children of God, partic-
ipating with God in the redemption of the world.

PRAYER

*Dear Spirit-God, we need the Spirit of forgiveness
toward the people who have hurt us, that we
might become more like Christ and have the bur-
den of our unforgiving sin cleansed from our
souls. We ask you, for our sakes, to answer Jesus'
prayer that we be forgiven. "Create in us a clean
heart, O God, and put a new and right spirit
within us." We offer our prayer in Jesus' name.
Amen.*

JESUS' SPIRIT—HUMILITY

Matthew 5:1–16   Philippians 2: 5–11
Micah 6:8

A favorite saint of many people is Francis of Assisi. The strength of Francis was his humility. Being humble in service to others, he reminds us of Jesus. Francis called his followers the "Friars Minor" to distinguish them from anything that might be considered "major." Even today, you may see a priest with these letters after his name: O.F.M. You know this person is a Franciscan and belongs to the "Order of Friars Minor."

The spirit of humility in Francis is captured in his well-known prayer: "O divine Master: Grant that I may not seek so much to be consoled, as to console; to be understood, as to understand; to be loved, as to love. For it is in giving that we receive; in pardoning that we are pardoned; and it is in dying that we are born to eternal life."

While working as an orderly in a hospital, one of my duties was to wash patients' feet. Have you ever washed anyone's feet other than your own? It is a humbling experience. The night before Jesus went to the cross, he shared with the disciples the spirit of their ministry; he went around the room and washed their feet. When they wanted to know who was the greatest, Jesus declared, "...the one who is servant of all" (Lk 22:26).

Micah declares: "What does the LORD require of you but to do justice, and to love kindness, and to walk humbly with your God?" (Mi 6:8).

Jesus said, "Let the children come to me, do not hinder them; for to such belongs the kingdom of God...whoever does not receive the kingdom of God like a child shall not enter it" (Mk 10:14–15). Does this mean that the humble, the meek, enter the kingdom before the sophisticated?

There is a profound life vitality in the spirit of humility. When we are humble we find strength to be witnesses for our Christ. There is an inner peace, too. Jesus says to us: "Take my yoke upon you, and learn from me; for I am gentle and lowly in heart, and you will find rest for your souls" (Mt 11:29).

Jesus sets forth his beatitudes for happiness: "Blessed are the poor in spirit;...blessed are the meek;...blessed are the merciful." We are to live humbly before Jesus, because he is the Christ—he is the vine and we are the branches. Without him we can do nothing.

The saving grace for any of us is the spirit of humility we receive from Jesus. The parable of the Pharisee and the Publican (tax collector) presents a vital truth. The Pharisee had done much good; no one could deny this. The tax collector had done much evil; he confessed his unworthiness. The difference: the Pharisee's spirit was that of self-centeredness; the spirit of the tax collector was that of humility before God, with a willingness to make restitution for his wrongs. The awesome presence of the Holy Spirit is for the humble.

Picture Jesus entering the city of God—riding humbly on a donkey. What is the Spirit of the Lord of life? The Bible sets before us the Spirit of Jesus, saying, "Though he was in the form of God, he did not count equality with God as something to be grasped; but, rather, emptied himself out, taking the form of a servant. He humbled himself and became obedient even unto death on a cross."

PRAYER

Lord God, help us to have the spirit of humility that was in Christ Jesus so we may "do nothing from selfishness or conceit; but in all humility count others better than ourselves." In Jesus' name—Amen.

IN LIFE AND IN DEATH, THE SPIRIT-GOD LEADS US

Luke 23:39–46

Jesus, hanging on the cross, savagely ridiculed by most of the people and about to give up his spirit, cries aloud to God, "Father, into thy hands I commit my spirit!" (Lk 23:46). God is Spirit, trustworthy, Holy Spirit. We are created in the image of God; somehow, our spirit is akin to the Spirit of God. The human Jesus, dying, expresses his utter trust in the Spirit-God.

In life, and in death: "All who are led by the Spirit of God are [children] of God. [I]t is the Spirit [of God] bearing witness with our spirit that we are children of God" (Rom 8:14, 16).

Suppose the almighty, creating, loving God, who presents himself to his created world as Holy Spirit, does so for many reasons. At least one of these is that he would like us to experience in this life what it truly means to be a trusting, human, child of God. Suppose the Spirit of God identifies with the human spirit to let us know that in our life and in our death, we are, in fact, cared-for children of the almighty, creating God, the beginning and the end.

The Holy Spirit, who, in the beginning, as he spoke, had life come into being, also participated in the birth of a child born in a cattle shed in a remote village. This child became the Savior of the world, the child of the living God. When this child came to die, he committed his life to the Spirit-God, who gave it to him in the beginning.

Isn't it possible that this same Holy Spirit also participated in our birth, is present in us and with us every moment? We, too, may be witnesses for the One who brought us into life. Doesn't the Spirit-God make his appeal through our spirits? When in any moment we experience the Holy Spirit present in our lives we can believe in the risen Jesus and in life eternal.

Where is God when we come to die? At death are we just abandoned to fade away into oblivion—or, can we, like Jesus, entrust our spirits to the eternal Spirit-God, whose love for us was real and present at our birth? Is not the saviorhood of Christ his ability to lead us in spirit and in truth to the very God who brought us into life? He tells one of the thieves on the cross, "Today, you will be with me in Paradise" (Lk 23:43).

The Scripture declares: "It is sown a physical body, it is raised a spiritual body." This is hard for us to fathom, but God will give us a body as it pleases him (1 Cor 15:38, 44).

Jesus, the Savior, on the cross, cries out to the eternal God. As frail children of dust, we, who trust Jesus, also cry out for the Holy Spirit-God to lead us each day of our lives and to be there with us when we come to die.

PRAYER

Dear Lord God, the facts of our birth and life are miracles to us. Our death is a huge fear and question mark. Help us to look to Jesus as our Savior. Help us, in our lifelong journey, to entrust our living to you; and when we come to die, may we, like Jesus, entrust our living spirits to you. We have faith that we are created in your image. We know that we need to be forgiven for our doubts and for the fears that consume our effective lives. Fill us with your Holy Spirit, O God, and lead us as your children in life and in death. We pray in the name and spirit of Jesus. Amen.

INVITING THE SPIRIT-GOD,
A STRANGER, INTO YOUR LIFE

1 Corinthians 2:9–13   John 3: 5–8
Ephesians 2:12–18

To know God more deeply than most of us do, we need to open our hearts and minds and invite the Holy Spirit of God to come in and take control.

When first we know the Spirit of God within us, he seems strange. It is like inviting a stranger in, one we do not know as well as we need to. Jesus said that the Spirit is like the wind, which blows where it wills. We do not know from whence it comes or where it is going. And surely we do not know where the Spirit will take us. This reality may well be something (Someone) we have never known before, never even dreamed of or imagined before.

In our day we have developed fears of those who are strangers—those who appear different from ourselves. They may hurt or use us. They may take the reins of power away from us.

In Jesus' day people found it difficult if not impossible to accept Jesus as a prophet because he came out of Galilee from the village of Nazareth. It was known that "no good could come out of Nazareth." He would become the heart of the redeemed life, but still we killed him. We today who think it odd that people could not accept this beautiful and wonderful Christ, still tend to reject those who come from a different place or background. In our day we are finding it easier to cross skin-pigment lines, but still find it difficult to cross or to intermingle cultural lines. We are inclined to say, "They would rather be with their own kind." We still shy away from those of a different faith or church because they appear to hold strange ideas sacred. However, when we open our hearts to them, to our delight, we find out wonderful things about God that we never knew we never knew.

The Bible tells us that the Spirit of God encourages us to be open to people differing from us. "You shall know the heart of a stranger, for you were strangers in the land of Egypt" (Ex 23:96). At first, even Jesus, the joyous, humble, loving Redeemer, seemed very strange or odd to us. Jesus said, "Come and inherit the kingdom, because I was a stranger and you welcomed me" (see Mt 25:34–35).

In the words of a hymn by Brian Wren, we sing:

> As Christ breaks bread and bids us share,
> each proud division ends.
> The love that made us makes us one,
> and strangers now are friends,
> and strangers now are friends.
> (© Hope Publishing Co.)

People who through their faith in Christ experience the inner presence of the Holy Spirit learn something about themselves and others—and about God that they never realized they never knew.

People have become excited and pleased by the golfing skills of the young man Tiger Woods—never before has any one of Afro-Asian-American heritage been a leader in the very competitive world of golf. And although Tiger Woods has risen to an unexpected high in athletics, he has, in an unusual manner, still maintained a personal humility, a thoughtfulness and a very caring spirit. We have come to know in Tiger Woods the person some wonderfully important things about human beings that many of us never knew.

Paul, in writing to the Ephesians, declares that the Holy Spirit of God, Stranger, is the presence who unites us with those from whom we have been estranged. "For he is our peace, who has made us both one....[F]or through him [Christ] we both have access in one Spirit to the Father" (Eph 2:14,18). He says, "For by one Spirit we were all baptized into one body....and all were made to drink of one Spirit" (1 Cor 12:13).

Jesus tells us that the Spirit is like a stranger. He is like the wind. You will never know where he will take you. When you invite this Stranger into your heart you learn things about God you never knew. "What no eye has seen, nor ear heard, nor the heart of a person conceived, what God has prepared for those who love him, God has revealed to us through the Spirit."

PRAYER

Dear Holy Spirit-God, come into my life now. I know many things I have learned along the way, but I need to know, I long to know, your Spirit presence. You are in many ways a Stranger to me. You cause me to be wary, uneasy; I do not know from whence you come or where you are going. I want to trust you, but I am afraid. May I travel with your Spirit? Come into my life and help me to know all the beauty, all the vitality, all the loveliness I can receive from you and you alone. Amen.

SPIRIT-GOD, RE-CREATOR

2 Corinthians 5:14–19   John 3: 1–8
Revelation 21:1–5

Life begins miraculously for us; we are created, male
and female, in the image of our Creator (Gn 1:27). The
human story, however, is full of our rebellion against
God, our violence toward each other, the behavior of
our sin-sick souls, our separations of will from the God
in whose image we are meant to be.

When the Spirit-God sends Jesus to be the Redeemer of
our lives, and the Savior, therefore, of the world, what is
it that God expects Jesus to do? Is it not to re-create us,
in the image of God, as we were meant to be? It is this
re-creating Spirit of God who gives us hope in our relationship with God and in our life together as humans.
For this reason, we are not to regard anyone, anymore
from our human point of view, but only from what each
person can become in Christ.

Our Scripture tells us that if anyone is "in Christ," that
person is a new creation. The old has passed away;

behold the new has come (2 Cor 5:17). To be in Christ is to be so immersed in Christ's love that the love of Christ controls us. It is in the re-creating love of God that we are to live and move and have our being. Therefore, we are to live no longer for ourselves, but for the sake of the one who died for us and who, for our sakes, was raised.

A highly intelligent, politically and religiously powerful person came to Jesus. He was a ruler of the Jews and a member of the Hebrew supreme court, the Sanhedrin. This religiously in-the-know person, Nicodemus, said something to Jesus. Do you remember what it was? He said, "Good Rabbi, we know that you are a teacher come from God; for no one can do these signs that you do, unless God is with him" (Jn 3:2). Do you see what Nicodemus meant? He was saying, "I am a deeply religious person, but, O Jesus, I long to have something of the God who is in you, in me." Jesus responded, "To experience the kingdom of God within, you must be born anew (from above, or again) of water (of repentance) and of the Spirit" (See Jn 3:3-5).

God is perfect love. How can we come expectantly into the kingdom of God as we are ordinarily? To be born again in the Spirit is essential. We need to long for and to pray that something of the God who was in Jesus also be in each of us.

We cannot re-create our own lives. We may try, make resolutions, change our ways, and this determination may help us. We may even be responding to the prevenient grace of the Holy Spirit touching our lives. But the Holy Spirit of God alone can re-create us. It is God in Christ reconciling the world to himself (2 Cor 5:19a).

In the ultimate salvation of our life together, we are told (Rev 21:1-5), there will be a new heaven and a new earth;

for the former things will pass away. It is the nature of God to continually create new life and to re-create those who have become estranged from his loving will.

The re-creating Spirit of God dwells within us, and we shall be his people. Presumably this means that once again we shall be in the image of God. God will wipe away every tear from our eyes, and our last enemy, death, shall be no more.

"[H]e who sat upon the throne said, 'Behold, I make all things new....Write this, for these words are trustworthy and true'" (Rev 21:5).

PRAYER

Dear Spirit God, our Creator and our Re-creator, we come humbly before you, confessing that we are sin-filled; we have tarnished severely your image in which we were created. We admit we suffer deeply from the evil of our estrangement from you. We strain, but, by ourselves, we are unable to recover. Our souls need to be re-created, reborn in your Spirit-image. You have beautiful and eternal possibilities for us. Please do not allow us to miss them. "Be thou our vision, O Lord of our hearts, naught be all else to us, save that thou art. Thou our best thought, by day or by night, waking or sleeping, thy presence our light." O Holy Spirit-God, re-create me, that I may be, in Christ, a new creation. May the love of Christ control me. May all of the old of me pass away, and all the new of thee become my life; in the name of Jesus, your Christ. Amen.
(Quotation, "Be though our vision...thy presence our light," is taken from an ancient Irish prayer translated by Mary E. Burne, 1905.)

THE WIND BLOWS WHERE IT WILLS

John 3:3–8, 14–15

"The wind blows where it wills, and you hear the sound of it, but you do not know whence it comes or whither it goes; so it is with every one who is born of the Spirit" (Jn 3:8). Is the Spirit of God whimsical? Are only the elite touched by the Wind of God?

Every one needs to be born anew in the Holy Spirit of God; we have no way to redeem ourselves. For it is not only that we cannot do good on our own, but we, by ourselves, cannot become good. "No one is good, but God alone" (Mk 10:18). We need the Wind of God to touch us. Our need is to be born anew in the Spirit of God, who alone is good. In our hope and expectation of eternal life, it is always, "Thanks be to God who gives us the victory through our Lord Jesus Christ" (1 Cor 15:57). We are saved by grace, the Wind of God that blows.

In his book, *The Person Reborn,* the Christian psychiatrist, Paul Tournier, declares, "Psychoanalysis explains a person's problems in order to bring them out into the daylight. The sunshine of God's grace dissolves them without our ever knowing exactly how" (p. 37).

Until our lives are reborn, we are restless, seeking a healing, a spiritual health, which only God's grace can provide for us. Without the Spirit of God we can even participate in evil without knowing that it is evil. We are restless and dissatisfied, longing to become children of God.

Reflect again: "The wind blows where it wills, and you hear the sound of it, but you do not know whence it comes or whither it goes; so it is with every one who is born of the Spirit" (Jn 3:8). The essence of God at work in our lives is *grace.*

The Wind of God, the grace of God, is not haphazard, and it is not by whim that the Spirit touches our lives. The Wind of God is love with a will for us. We find rebirth by our baptism in the water of repentance—our sorrow that we have fallen short of God's glory. We find our rebirth by coming to Jesus, believing that he is of God. We come to our rebirth by inviting Jesus to come into our lives as our Lord and Christ. "As Moses lifted up the serpent in the wilderness, so must the Son of man be lifted up, that whoever believes in him may have eternal life" (Jn 3:14–15). It is by water and the Wind of God that we are reborn.

It is only as we are born again in the Spirit that we become valid witnesses for the lordship of our Christ. The Christian Church is not just an organization. It is a fellowship of people, reborn in the Spirit, who are reaching out to share with others their new life.

PRAYER

Dear Spirit-God, you are not whimsical about our life with you. You do love each one of us as though there were only one of us to love. Help us to love you with our total being. Enable us to open our spirit-lives to you and to experience a deep spiritual rebirth. We give thanks to you that you are searching for us and longing for us to become one with you in spirit and in truth. We believe that, as we allow the Holy Spirit to transform and lead us, we learn your will for us. Help us to let go of all false securities and to entrust our total being to you, O Wind of God. Amen.

PENTECOST, THE BIRTH OF THE CHURCH

Acts 2:1-4; 14-47

People thought they were drunk. Why not? These, rather poor, uninteresting people had become alive and excited. These passive disciples had now suddenly become enthusiastic apostles. It all happened on Pentecost (a Hebrew holiday)—the birth of the church of Jesus Christ our Lord. I suppose you would call this "prevenient grace." No one told God to do it; no one had ever envisioned it; so no one expected God to do it. For some unknown reason, God, in love and mercy, poured out his Holy Spirit upon some unlikely Galileans. They had, for three years, followed Jesus as their teacher and after experiencing his resurrection and ascension had gathered in one place. In that moment with the outpouring of God's Holy Spirit, people were called to witness for the risen Christ, and the church was born.

They said there was a sound like a mighty wind; they did not know from whence it came or where it was going. They certainly did not know where it would take them! It came without human calling; no one could have envisioned it. Red flashes like tongues of fire appeared to rest on the heads of these new apostles. Surely God was expecting miraculous things from them. God sent Jesus so that we, believing in him, would be baptized with the Holy Spirit and with fire.

Peter began to preach with great fervor and enthusiastic power about the meaning of the risen Christ to the world. In seminary we used to sing a song with words like these: "O crucified and risen Lord, give tongues of fire to preach thy Word." Certainly God did not do this just to make certain that people looked pretty or odd. They were given tongues of fire to become the church, to preach the Word—to take the word of the crucified and risen Lord to the sin-sick and fear-filled world. It was never expected that any good could come out of Galilee, but, in this moment, even foreigners could understand what these Galilean fishermen were saying. Pentecost tells us that God pours out his Holy Spirit upon us so we, in a deeper way, may witness to God's presence in our lives.

Peter reminded them of the words of Joel, the prophet (Jl 2:28–32). The church of Jesus the Christ is born when people begin to see visions and to dream dreams of the kingdom of God. The church is born when they begin to call on the name of the Lord to save them, empower them and send them forth to tell the world of the risen Lord. The church comes alive when people give themselves to the mission of God's Holy Spirit.

PRAYER

O holy God, in your Spirit we become the church. Too often we have been content to sit in our pews without allowing your Spirit to take control of our souls. We ask your forgiveness. Grant us to become

Pentecost people in whom your Holy Spirit dwells. Fill us, O God! Show us your purpose. Empower us to work together in your Spirit, without haste and without ceasing, until your kingdom comes to our hearts and to the heart of the whole world. Amen.

THE CHURCH AND THE HOLY SPIRIT

1 Corinthians 12:1–13   Ephesians 1:15–23

The church is an *ecclesia,* a fellowship of faithful people, called out by the Holy Spirit of God to be witnesses for the living Christ. No one can say: "Jesus is Lord!" except by the Holy Spirit. They believe that to experience Jesus as Lord, deep within their souls, is the richest possible blessing, coming only from the one true God.

For them, it is a sacrament when, as a fellowship of believing people, they break bread and drink the cup of sacrifice together. As they remember the Lord Jesus, they personally experience the grace of God. These are people who realize that it is a true sacrament for them to be baptized and for their children to be promised to God as they, too, are baptized.

The church is a gathering of those who confess their sins and who ask forgiveness from the mercy of God revealed to them in the crucified and risen Lord. They offer forgiveness for even their enemies and others who have hurt them. They believe the crucified Lord has already forgiven their enemies, and they are committed to bearing witness to the Spirit of Christ abiding in their hearts.

The church is a people who have received the gifts of the Holy Spirit and know these gifts are to be used for the "common good." All are blessed as they share the greatest gift of all, the agape love of God, in caring for one another. They realize they are the church, the body of Christ, the people in whom the life of the Holy Spirit dwells. They know that the church is founded on a "rock," lives committed to Jesus as the Christ, the Son of the living God (Mt 16:18). It was in the indwelling of the Spirit of Christ, the Holy Spirit, that the church was born. There would have been no church, no Christian community, had not the promised Holy Spirit been given.

They are a witnessing *koinonia* fellowship who believe they will be judged ultimately by whether or not they have fed the hungry, clothed the naked, given a drink of water to the thirsty and visited the sick and the imprisoned. They are people empowered by the Holy Spirit in ministry. They believe the Lordship of Christ is essential to determine the very spirit with which they live and the kind of persons they are.

The church is reborn people, baptized by the Holy Spirit, who experience the grace all people need and yearn for. Central in the heart of the Church is the "fire" of the Holy Spirit bringing love, joy, peace of mind and a certitude that God is alive in human life.

The church is a fellowship of people who have given their lives to Christ, and who believe the presence of the Holy Spirit is the risen Christ, alive with them forever.

PRAYER (anonymous)

Thy body, broken for my sake, my bread from heaven shall be; Thy testamental cup I take and thus remember thee. Remember thee and all thy pain and all thy love for me. Yea, while yet a breath, a pulse remain, I will remember thee. When these failing lips grow dumb and mind and memory flee, when thou shalt in thy kingdom come, O Lord, remember me. Amen.

CALLED TO BAPTIZE IN THE NAME OF...
THE HOLY SPIRIT

Matthew 28:16–20

One of the difficulties with being a Christian is that it sometimes seems impossible to live up to what, in our relationship to Christ, we believe this God of Jesus wants us to be.

Those first disciples were as unsure as we are about whether they could indeed live the Christian life in the kind of world where people stoned the prophets and crucified the Lord of life. We usually feel, along with the apostle Paul, that "I do not do the good I want, but the evil I do not want is what I do" (Rom 7:19). Who doesn't feel this way, at least, some of the time?

Missionaries going out in the "name of Christ" to win converts have quoted again and again our Scripture text, Matthew 28:16–20. In my reading of the Bible when anything is done in the "name of Jesus," or in the "name of God," the word *name* implies "authority" or "power," more particularly, "spiritual power."

With this in mind, we consider this text, in which Jesus is now risen from the dead and about to ascend into heaven; he says that all authority in heaven and on earth has been given to him. One manuscript says that the disciples prostrated themselves on the ground and worshiped him. Even though Jesus had been crucified and risen from the dead, still some doubted that all authority in the world had been given to him. Though he was standing there, perhaps some even doubted that he had indeed been raised from the dead. Some, perhaps, doubted they would be able to go out into that cruel, violent, greedy world and ever win any converts. So Jesus tries to tell them and us what to do.

In essence, Jesus says to those people, to you and to me, to all who would like to win others to Jesus: "Go forth, go forth into all the world, including the unbelieving, unfaithful, ungodly world and baptize people in the power of God, the power of the risen Son, the power of the Holy Spirit presence in your life; and I will be with you always."

You can't win converts to Jesus the Christ by your good looks or by your charisma or by your hard work; you can do it only by the power of the Holy Spirit in your human life. It is this presence of the Holy Spirit that gives you the genuineness, the courage and the spiritual stamina to stand up and win others to the Christ who lives within you.

PRAYER

Dear Holy Spirit-God, I am afraid to go out on my own to speak for Christ. I do not speak very well, and I am not very brave. I surrender much too easily to the world and its ways. If I am to baptize others, I will need your Spirit vitality. I will need to be baptized myself in thy Holy Spirit. How can I baptize anyone in the name of the Father, and the Son and the Holy Spirit if I have not the authority of thy holy presence within? I know that anything I can do, I can do only in the "name" of thy Spirit. Amen.

ACEDIA VS. PARACLETE

Isaiah 61:1–3   John 14:15–17
John 14:25–27   John 15:8–11

In talking with some young people, I asked them about their worship experience. They responded, "We don't go; it is boring."

A young Jewish girl who had lived in Israel for four years, declaring she was truly religious, said she was going to return to Israel after she finished her schooling. In reply to my question about which synagogue she attended, she said that she did not go to synagogue very often; it was boring.

There is a word, "acedia," which means spiritual boredom. Some theologians attribute this word to some early church fathers who went into the desert to "fight evil." However, they became somewhat indifferent to sacred matters and increasingly lazy. Carlyle Marney, speaking to seminary students, asked them if they thought that in ten years they would still love the Lord Jesus, or whether they would become "hand tamed by the gentry"? None of the students believed they would change. The fact is that many succumbed to acedia in their work.

Whatever happens to those who have experienced the Holy Spirit and know in their hearts "a garland instead of ashes, the oil of gladness instead of mourning, the mantle of praise instead of a faint spirit" (Is 61:3) — those who seem to be the planting of the Lord to display his glory? What happened to Jesus' promise that our joy might be full—and to our promise to glorify God and to enjoy him forever?

Indifference comes when one feels that the efforts put forth for good most often are ineffective and wasted. To try to live a spirited or joyous life is unreal. Why try?

John uses another word, *Paraclete,* which means the Holy Spirit as "comforter" or "advocate." The word, comforter, comes from a Latin word meaning "brave." Thus the Comforter is one who enables some dispirited person to be brave or strong in the face of trouble. Our Scripture declares that the Paraclete, the Holy Spirit, brings a comfort and a peace, even a peace which passes our understanding—one which the world cannot know. In the Holy Spirit, in this comforting experience of God's soul-calming peace, we receive something we all long for. This does not mean we are indifferent or spiritually bored. Life in the Holy Spirit is meant to be peaceful, joyful, excited about being full and eternally alive in Christ—yes, but not bored or indifferent.

In our worship times with the Holy Spirit, we realize that, indeed, the risen Christ is with us. Our hearts sing the "Hallelujah Chorus": "He is king of kings, he is Lord of Lords." The love and joy and peace of the Paraclete are real. Spiritual boredom is spiritual indifference, doubt, even fear and, consequently, an alienation from God. Repenting our lack of faith in the risen Lord, and inspired by our belief, we come to experience the Holy Spirit as courage and indescribable peace and joy—and this holds exciting possibilities for us.

PRAYER

God, remove our acedia, and have the Holy Spirit fill our praise worship with joy. With the Holy Spirit, may we be strong and brave in a spirited witness for Christ. Amen.

DRIVEN BY THE SPIRIT

Mark 1:9–13   Ephesians 3:1–8

There is a story in Second Samuel that raises a poignant question for us. The story is that the Hebrew people were in a fierce battle with such a formidable enemy they did not expect to win, but they did! They were so jubilant about winning that they wanted to send the message of the victory back home to the king, whose very life depended on their winning. The only way they had of sending messages was by runners. The general, Joab, had two outstanding runners, one of whom wanted especially to carry the news. But, alas, the general chose the other runner. The disappointed runner went to the general and asked if he could run along with the one who carried the tidings. The general said to the disappointed runner, "Why do you run, my son, since you have no message?"

What is your message? What keeps you running? What drives your life?

In the gospel of Mark, when Jesus was baptized, the

Holy Spirit "drove" him into the wilderness to confront his temptations. As a consequence, Jesus realized that people do not live by bread alone, but by every word that proceeds out of the mouth of God. He declared that one should worship only God, and this God alone should people serve. To confront us with our serving of lesser gods, I believe the Holy Spirit drives us to face our temptations.

The Spirit of God is love. Because the Spirit is love, we are driven by the Spirit to be loving. Any attempt on our part to be other than loving is always self-defeating.

Our sincere response to the God who created us is both inward and outward, both inner devotion and tending to human need. The spiritual drive of your life begins on the inside and then moves to the outside. The Spirit of God driving you is essential for you to serve unselfishly those you love and the others around you with human needs.

Paul is driven by the Holy Spirit to bring the gospel to the Gentiles—something others did not want to do. Writing to the Ephesians, he tells them the Spirit of God has revealed that the Gentiles are, also, eligible to be a part of the body of Christ. He says, "Of this gospel I was made a minister according to the gift of God's grace [Holy Spirit] which was given me by the working of his power" (3:7). "Woe to me if I do not preach the gospel" (1 Cor 9:16).

Martin Luther, before the Diet of Worms, putting his life on the line for his conviction that salvation is by faith, declares: "Here I stand, I can do no other." The Holy Spirit drives us in our faithfulness to God.

PRAYER

O Lord God, fill us with your grace, your Holy Spirit. Give us a message we can share with our families, others around us and even our enemies. Drive us by your Spirit to confront our temptations to serve lesser gods. Grant us the spirit to live for you. Amen.

YOU ARE A TEMPLE OF THE HOLY SPIRIT

1 Corinthians 3:16–17	1 Corinthians 6:17–20
2 Corinthians 6:16	Ephesians 2:19–22
2 Timothy 1:11–14	

Paul writes to Timothy, his child in the gospel: "I am not ashamed, for I know whom I have believed....Follow the pattern...which you have heard from me, in the faith and love which are in Christ Jesus; guard the truth that has been entrusted to you by the Holy Spirit who dwells within us" (2 Tm 1:12–14). An undeniable reality is the life of the Holy Spirit within you.

Can you believe that the truth of God entrusted to you is indeed the holy presence of the God who loved you into life?

For the Hebrew people, the Temple was the abiding place of the God who made them a special people. The thought of our lives being temples of the Holy Spirit is indeed a sacred and lovely analogy. Paul says, "You are God's Temple, and that Temple is holy." We are not to be immoral or ill-spirited people, because we are not to sin against the God whose Holy Spirit dwells within us.

Paul says, in 1 Corinthians 2:1–5, "When I came to you...I did not come proclaiming to you the testimony of God in lofty words or wisdom...I was with you in weakness and in much fear and trembling; and my speech and my message were not in plausible words of wisdom, but in demonstration of the Spirit and of the power, that your faith might not rest in [human] wisdom, but in the power of God."

The power of any person's witness is not his or her ability to speak fluently, but the presence of the Holy Spirit in that person's life.

It is nice to be able to tell others how we enjoy the love and joy and peace of God ourselves—but words do not convince. In a deep mystical way God's presence within us is our only witness. You cannot persuade others that God loves them unless they know you love them. We do not, and cannot, manufacture the qualities other people need. They are the fruit of God's Holy Spirit presence. People know this instinctively.

It is one of the deeper mysteries of the Christian experience, that the Spirit leads and interprets spiritual truths to those who possess the Spirit. This is the witness of Christians: "We are God's temple and God's Spirit dwells in us."

PRAYER

Dear Lord God, we know it is through our faith in Jesus as the Christ that your Holy Spirit gains entrance to our lives. This is our salvation—your grace received through our faith. O Lord God, do not leave us alone. Without you we are empty and meaningless. We know that we are created to be temples of your Holy Spirit. It is through the Holy Spirit that we gain certitude of you. Your presence within is our witness for you. Thank you, Lord, for living in us. Amen.

ONE IN THE SPIRIT

John 4:7–15, 23–24   Acts 4:30–33
1 Corinthians 12:12–14

When a Samaritan woman came to Jacob's well where Jesus was resting, he asked her for a drink of water. You may recall that the Jews, for hundreds of years, had had no dealings with the Samaritans. Because of this, and the fact that she was a woman, the Samaritan woman was startled that a Jewish man might even speak to her, let alone ask her for the favor of a drink of water.

This is a deeply caring scene, and the beginning of our insight into the universality of God's redeeming love for all people. We have a hard time understanding God who so loved that he sent Jesus—and not just to us and ours. Jesus reveals to this Samaritan woman the love of God for each of us, whosoever we might be.

Jesus tells her that if she were to ask him, he would give her a drink of "living water." The woman, I think, did not understand what Jesus meant, but, nevertheless, asked for that kind of water. The invitation to come to

Jesus and receive living water is for the world. Without Christ our souls thirst for God, and our souls would like to drink of the water of eternal life. Jesus is saying that he gives to us what our souls long for. He says this even to the Samaritan woman, thought by Jesus' people to be a hopeless outsider, shut out from God.

Eternal life is a grace-full gift of God. Certainly no one is worthy of the living water. We are reconciled through the Spirit of Christ to our Creator. We are made one with each other in our common need for the Holy Spirit of God, and in our souls' longing for the life which is eternal. It is the Spirit of Christ in each of us, reaching out to care, that makes us one with each other.

In this context, the words of the Peter Scholtes song ring true:

> We are one in the Spirit.
> We are one in the Lord....
> And they'll know we are Christians by our love,...
> Yes they'll know we are Christians by our love.

No one can say freely, "Jesus is Lord!" except by the Holy Spirit. We are the church of Jesus Christ when, one in the agape Spirit of God, we proclaim together, "Jesus is Lord!" "[J]ust as the body is one and has many members, and all the members of the body, though many, are one body, so it is with Christ. For by one Spirit we were all baptized into one body—Jews or Greeks, slave or free—and all were made to drink of one Spirit" (1 Cor 12:12–13).

When we come to Christ, the grace-full Holy Spirit of God is the "living water," welling up within each of us, making us one with each other forever. Acts tells us that those who believed were filled with the Holy Spirit and were of one heart and soul (see 4:31–32).

PRAYER

Take more than a few moments to invite the Holy Spirit to come into your life and to be the "living water" of eternal life for you and for all those around you, even those with whom you have no dealings.

PRAYING IN THE SPIRIT

Ephesians 6:13–18   Jude 20, 21

To pray in the Spirit is to allow the Holy Spirit to take over your spirit life, allowing the Spirit to inspire, energize and sustain you as you pray.

Paul, in a Roman prison where it was only permissible to declare "Caesar is Lord," proclaims "Christ is Lord." He knows that no one can do this without the Holy Spirit. He lives and prays in the Spirit of Christ in an ugly-spirited, secular, Roman world. He tells the Ephesians to remain faithful to Christ's Spirit; for, he declares, only as they pray in the Spirit will they be effective in dealing with the evil in the world and with the sin in themselves.

Praying in the Spirit is initiated by the Holy Spirit of God. It is God's grace touching our lives, blessing us and transforming us. Praying in the Spirit is allowing the Spirit to pray through us, reaching out to God in our behalf and in behalf of those for whom we are praying.

To pray in the Spirit is to pray in the Spirit of the God revealed to us in Jesus the Christ. We are praying in the

Spirit when we allow the Spirit of God to lead and mold, and empower all we are, as Jesus the Christ did.

God is Spirit, not just any kind of spirit, but a sacrificing, forgiving Spirit. When we pray in the Spirit, we remember Jesus' prayer in the Garden of Gethsemane. He is full of the abundant life. He faces death. He clearly does not want to die. The cup is a symbol of sacrifice. He prays that, if possible, God might take away the cup, but that, nevertheless, he wants God's will to be done. In his prayer Jesus allows the Spirit of God to determine his way. It is not easy. To give his life for the salvation of the sinful world is sheer sacrifice.

The Spirit in our prayer expresses the love of God toward those for whom we are interceding. When we pray in the Spirit, there is no self; there is only God's love. In my own prayer life, sometimes I quiet myself before God. I want the Spirit of God to come into my total being, body, mind and soul, to heal me, to bring a new spiritual vitality to my whole life. As I pray for myself, I find my prayer interrupted by the remembrance of others who also need healing or a special blessing of God's love. I realize I need to stop thinking about myself and to pray for others. I begin to pray for them as I might have prayed for myself. The consequence is that I believe myself to be more nearly healed than when I simply pray for myself.

Praying in the Spirit often stimulates almost overwhelming emotion, love for God, love for others. It often brings Spirit-motivated activity. Some people hold their arms in the air, generally with open hands so that they may not miss anything God, in that sacred moment, is offering to them. It is powerful prayer when the Spirit of God prays through us, bringing the joy of God's presence in our prayer.

To pray in the Spirit is to pray with abandonment, forgetting self, praying with sacrificial love and praising the Lord.

PRAYER

Dear Holy Spirit-God, we praise you every day of our lives for Jesus, who drank of the cup of sacrifice for our sakes. We pray that your will may be done in our lives, as it was in Jesus' life. Fill us with your Holy Spirit and help us to pray in your Spirit, even as Jesus prayed. Amen.

WORSHIPING IN THE SPIRIT

John 4:23–24   Psalm 150

"O come, let us sing to the Lord;...[L]et us worship and bow down, let us kneel before the Lord, our Maker" (Ps 95:1, 6).

Some people feel they must worship in a certain building, or with a certain denomination, so they may participate in sacramental experience. I asked a person from another denomination whether the communion service would mean anything if I administered the elements to him. He said clearly, "No!" This seemed strange to me because worshiping together in the Holy Spirit of God knits people together in a special wholeness and oneness with each other.

In our Scripture meditation, the Samaritan woman reminds Jesus that her people have worshiped in the right place, that is, on the mountain in Samaria, while Jesus' people have declared that Jerusalem was the only true place to worship. It was then Jesus said to the

Samaritan woman, "God is spirit, and those who worship him must worship in spirit and truth" (Jn 4:24).

A person believing in Christ becomes a temple in whom the Holy Spirit of God resides. In one sense a person's inner experience of the Holy Spirit is the only certitude that person has of the reality of the God he or she is worshiping. It is in gratitude for this inner presence that the worshiper receives the broken bread and the poured-out wine of the sacrament.

Yet it is, probably, this idea of worshiping God in Spirit that divides many congregations from one another. Some feel that only those who speak in tongues are truly Christian. Some on the opposite end of the spectrum feel they cannot do anything in a worship service not printed in the bulletin. Worshiping in the Spirit is praising the Lord's presence with one's whole being.

C. S. Lewis used to say: "We go to a worship service to enact it. Good reading becomes possible only when you do not think about your eyes, the light, the print or the spelling. The perfect worship service would be one in which we are aware of nothing else, but God." We come to worship to express our love for God.

In worship the only truth is the Spirit. The Bible tells us, "What no eye has seen, nor ear heard, nor the heart of man conceived, what God has prepared for those who love him, God has revealed to us through the Spirit" (1 Cor 2:9–10). We are even told to pray in the Spirit, because no one comprehends the thought of God, except the Spirit of God (1 Cor 2:11). To worship God in Spirit is to become empowered with spiritual insights we have not previously known. The Holy Spirit, then, becomes the informing, guiding, motivating, presence in our worship.

To worship in Spirit is to surrender our self-centeredness and allow the Spirit to take control of our mind and spirit. Long for your spirit to become more like the Spirit of Jesus. When we worship in Spirit we give thanks, praise and glory to the God who resides in us.

PRAYER

Praise the Lord. Praise the Lord in his sanctuary. Praise him with songs and prayers. Let everything that breathes praise the Lord. Praise the Lord. Amen.

CONFESSING THAT JESUS IS THE SON OF GOD

1 John 4:1–15

This is one of the most beautiful passages in the whole Bible. It reveals that God is Spirit, and that God's Spirit is love. No one has ever seen God, but when we love one another, we know that the one true God abides in us.

We are physical and spiritual beings. We always want to be physically healthy, but we are not always aware of the importance of our spirit. We sometimes accept an ungodly or mean spirit as a "given" that cannot be healed or changed. We feel it is just the way humans are created to be. We are challenged to test the spirit of our lives to see whether or not we are of God.

When Jesus and the disciples traveled to Caesarea Philippi, a Roman stronghold, Jesus asked the disciples, "Who do you say that I am?" (Mt 16:15). Peter spoke up and, in a startled sort of way, said, "You are the Christ, the Son of the living God" (Mt 16:16). All Christians are called upon to make their confession that Jesus is the Son of God.

Jesus is Emmanuel, the Love-Spirit in our midst (God with us). His life and teachings reveal the very nature of God to us. When he reaches out to someone or heals someone, he does it with love for that person, that the Love-God may be glorified. When we see this love in Jesus, then we know that Jesus is the Son of God.

Our Scripture calls on us to confess that Jesus is the Messiah for us. He alone reveals to us what it means to be fully alive. When we come to believe that Jesus is the Son of the living God, we ourselves become children of God.

We confess that Jesus is the Son of God, when we, in fact, believe that Jesus' love is the Spirit of God. When we begin each day praying that the Spirit of God in Jesus will empower us to love, Jesus becomes the Messiah for us.

In our world we see all kinds of treachery, unfaithfulness, violence, hatred and spiritual sickness. We confess that Jesus is the Son of God when we realize that the Spirit of Jesus in us is stronger and more life-determining than the admitted power of evil in the world.

Our confession of Jesus as the Christ of our lives must come in our words, but even more as we share the love of God with each other. The world can be full of hate, cruelty and violence and worship other gods, but we cannot. Our words, our lives confess that, for us, Jesus is Lord, the Son of the living God.

PRAYER

Dear Lord God, we are deeply grateful that you have sent Jesus to be the expiation for our sins, even the sins of the spirit, and that in confessing him as our Lord, we become your spirit-children. Sometimes our spirits are ugly or mean or rude, unacceptable even to ourselves. Cleanse us, heal us, grant us rebirth in your Holy Spirit. Redeem our spirit-lives that we may belong to you, and be vital witnesses for Jesus, now and forever. Amen.

SPIRITUAL GIFTS FOR THE "COMMON" GOOD

1 Corinthians 12:1–13

The God in Christ said to us, "I will build my church" (Mt 16:18). Our Scripture meditation tells us that the Lord provides us spiritual gifts to be used in building the church and to carry out his ministry in our midst. We are reminded that each Christian has at least one gift; some have more than one; and no one has them all.

The gifts of the Spirit are just that. They are not something that we earn or deserve, but gifts that the Holy Spirit of God has chosen to give to us (Heb 2:4).

God's spiritual gifts to us are not for any self-chosen or selfish purpose, nor does a spiritual gift prove that the receiver is especially holy or in some way closer to God. The spiritual gifts are from God for the common good. God provides the gifts as he chooses, to build up the church, the body of Christ.

If you have a spiritual gift or gifts, you are blessed, because you know that God has included you to have a part in his ministry. It does not mean you must have a certain gift (e.g., speaking in tongues), before you are acceptable to God.

I believe that gifted people have a special purpose to carry out for God. It is important to pray about your gift(s) so that you use them for God's intended purpose.

Some people with the gift to be plumbers are preachers, and some people with the gift to be preachers are plumbers. (No gift is higher or holier than another.) Some people without the gift of teaching try to teach, and some people with the gift for teaching fail to participate in the teaching ministry. Spiritual vitality comes into our lives as we use our spiritual gifts for the "common good," to build the church.

God is Spirit. His gifts to us are spiritual gifts; they are not just human talents. Because we are talented with creative ideas does not mean that we can build the church of God. God will build the church, or it will be just another human institution. He will use us and our gifts according to his idea and will.

A spiritual gift is a sacred trust given to us by a God who loves us and who wants us to participate in his ministry as it pleases him. We need to pray about the gifts we have or wish to have, and then to allow ourselves to be used as the Holy Spirit directs.

PRAYER

Dear Spirit-God, we bless you for our spiritual gifts. We are glad that you have chosen us to be a part of your ministry and to contribute to the "common good." We know that the church of Jesus Christ is the people who, in their faith, entrust their lives to the Christ. We pray that you will increase our courage that we may be open to your Holy Spirit. We long to be a guided fellowship of faithful people. May we have the insight to help one another, and especially our children, to discern the spiritual gifts that you have given us. We pray in the name of the Father and of the Son and of the Holy Spirit. Amen.

THE GREATEST SPIRITUAL GIFT

1 Corinthians 12:27–31   1 Corinthians 13

Most of us dream of being better persons than we are. We long to be more deeply spiritual. Our false gods are worthless in this longing. We come on our knees before the God of Jesus, praying that we might be reborn in his Spirit.

It was my privilege just the other day to lead a worship service in a health-care unit. Some came in wheel chairs. Some slept most of the time. I wondered what would make any difference to these infirm people. We sang some favorite hymns (one verse each). We read some of their favorite Scriptures. Then I went around the room and knelt before each person, holding their hands and praying that this person might know that God loved him or her and wanted all of them there to love each other. Tears ran down their faces as I prayed. Following my prayers, tears ran down my face as we sang "Jesus loves me, this I know."

We are taught (1 Cor 12:31) that our search is for the higher spiritual gifts; there is a more excellent way of being fully alive. What is more, most spiritual gifts in the normal course of life will pass away. Speaking in tongues, without love, will sound like a clanging cymbal. If a person has prophetic powers, understands all mysteries and all knowledge and has the faith to remove mountains, but has no love, that person is really nothing.

The gift of love is essential before all other gifts, because all others are imperfect and will pass away. The gift of love is necessary that we may give up our childish ways and come to see ourselves clearly.

God is love, but not just any kind. God is agape, sacrificial love. In our behalf God bears all things, believes all things, hopes all things and endures all things. This kind of love never ceases. This gift will hold you up and heal you and inspire you always. In our time, for me, Mother Teresa was the personification of God's love. She declared that Jesus came to teach us how to love, and that "Each person is to love others as Jesus loved."

This Holy Spirit gift is unique, because it is the Love-God giving himself to us. It is the Holy Spirit coming to abide forever in our spirits.

Several gifts given to us abide: faith and hope and love; but surely the greatest gift of all is the Love-God giving us of his own Spirit, to be for us a more excellent way. The love the Spirit-God in Christ gives to us, is the only truly enduring gift.

Our need is to long for and to pray for this higher gift, for this more excellent eternal way of life.

PRAYER

Dear Holy Spirit-God, we pray to you, because without you we are like the chaff which the wind drives away. We pray for spiritual gifts that we may indeed participate in your ministry. But, O Lord, we long for a more excellent way of life. We believe that we are created to live eternal lives. We ask that you will provide us with the gifts of faith and hope; they are true blessings to us. We kneel before you and confess that without your love-presence we are really nothing, and, try as we may on our own, we remain nothing. We sincerely pray that you will give your Holy Spirit-Self to us. We beseech you for the greatest spiritual gift: thyself, O God; in the name of Jesus Christ our Lord. Amen.

THE FRUIT OF THE SPIRIT
(Love, Joy, Peace, Patience, Kindness, Goodness,
Faithfulness, Gentleness, Self-Control)

Galatians 5:16–24   Psalm 1
Matthew 7:17–20

The Psalmist instructs us saying that each one who med-
itates on the law of the Lord shall be like a strong "tree
planted by streams of water, that yields its fruit in its
season" (Ps 1:2-3).

Jesus teaches us that there is a difference between "good
fruit" and "evil fruit." Indeed, an evil tree cannot bring
forth good fruit, and a good tree cannot bring forth evil
fruit. We are known by the fruit we bear. Evil fruit is as
harmful to us and others as good fruit is a blessing. Evil
is an ungodly spirit, seemingly so natural that we come
to believe it is acceptable. Note some qualities of evil
that Paul lists: jealousy, strife, envy, selfishness, drunk-
enness, idolatry.

In a real way the presence of God's Holy Spirit is the
strength of our character. It is evidenced by our ability

to love people who do not like us and to sacrifice one's own life for the sake of others. The Christian is one whose life is sustained by the Spirit of Christ. The presence of this Holy Spirit brings into our lives the Spirit-fruit that we come to realize is all we long for in life. Read again the fruit of the Spirit: love, joy, peace, patience, kindness, goodness, faithfulness, gentleness, self-control. This Spirit-fruit presence is true evidence that we know Christ.

A ninety-two-year-old man's wife was seriously ill. She had been in the hospital for a number of weeks and then came home. This ninety-two-year-old man cared night and day for his wife a long time before she died. When I visited him and his wife, I asked him, "Bruce, how can you stand this hard trial?" He replied, "When we were married, I promised to love her until death do us part; and I plan to do just that." "The fruit of the Holy Spirit is: love...faithfulness...."

We find the Holy Spirit and, consequently, the fruit of the Spirit, coming into our lives through our faith in Jesus as the Christ. Jesus teaches, "I am the vine and you are the branches. Abide in me, and I in you. Apart from me you can do nothing. A branch by itself cannot bring forth fruit; neither can you, except you abide in me. By this my Father is glorified, when you bear much fruit" (Jn 15:4–5).

The church is not just the people who gather within the walls of a special building on a Sabbath morning. The church is the people empowered by the Holy Spirit. We glorify God when we manifest the fruit of the Spirit in our lives. This is a true witness that we are, indeed, the "ecclesia," the called of God, summoned to serve him.

PRAYER

Dear Lord, You are the bread of life for us. You are eternal life within us. Nothing else matters. Fill us, Holy Spirit. We pray we may bear your fruit, for Jesus' sake and ours. Amen.

FRUIT OF THE SPIRIT—LOVE

Matthew 5:43–48   Galatians 5:22–23
1 John 3:14–18

Early on a cold winter morning after a snowfall of about one and a half feet, I saw an angel. She came walking down the middle of the road, apparently because it was too difficult to walk on the snow-covered walks. I was out early and had already shoveled my own walk, my sick neighbor's walk and the walk of the widow next door by the time she arrived. She looked at the walks I had shoveled and then down the long street of yet unshoveled walks. Without slowing down, she asked very quietly as she passed: "How far does your love go?" This is the kind of question only an angel could ask.

How far does your love go? It goes only as far as the strength of God's love within will take you. Love is the fruit of God's Holy Spirit presence.

The "good news" is that we are not able to love on our own, but that God first loved us, and then we loved.

"God's love has been poured into our hearts through the Holy Spirit which has been given to us" (Rom 5:5).

It has been observed that the unique teaching of Jesus is to love our enemies and to pray for the people who would hurt us. No one, either before Jesus or since Jesus, has ever taught this. Why should we love people who would persecute us? Jesus tell us that we are to do this so that we may become children of God and perfect in love as God is perfect in love. It is God's presence that enables us to love as God loves.

God's love, present in us, is our salvation; it alone qualifies us to be compared with angels. Other people realize that we are disciples of Jesus only when we care for them with God's love. Of the few things that truly last in life, the greatest of these is God's love. We pass from death to life when we love each other as Christ has loved us (See 1 Jn 3:14). We pass from death to life only when the fruit of God's Spirit within us loves through us.

Tagore of India once said to people in India striving to become Christian: "On a spiritual plane you cannot do good until you are good. You cannot preach Christianity until you have Christ, and then you will not preach 'Christianity,' but the God who is love, as Christ did."

To love as Christ loves is a victory over self. William Barclay says: "The plain fact is that Christian love is the fruit of the Spirit....This is why it is futile to think about the world accepting the ethics of the Sermon on the Mount or of Christian love. The truth is that the world cannot accept them; only the Spirit-filled, Christ-devoted Christian can. It is something which is quite impossible without the dynamic of Jesus Christ" (*The Letters to the Galatians and Ephesians* [Daily Study Bible Series], Philadelphia: Westminster Press, 1976).

Again, it is Barclay who says: "God's love is great for three reasons: it loved us when we were dead in our sin; it quickens us to a new life in which we can love others; and it never ends."

PRAYER

O Lord God, your life-giving reality is known by your life-changing love for us and within us. We know that your love is not just any superficial, cheap feeling, but agape, sacrificial love. It is the only power strong enough to change us and to redeem the world. Our moral and spiritual strengths come from your love within us. We have character, courage and hope, only when your love is poured out upon us by your Holy Spirit. Thank you, O Lord, our God. Amen.

FRUIT OF THE SPIRIT—JOY

Galatians 5:22 –23   John 15:8–11
Luke 2:8–14   Romans 14:17

The most beautiful story in the Bible is the story of the birth of Jesus, which begins with an angel appearing to the shepherds on a hillside outside the village of Bethlehem. They were afraid. The angel said to them, "Do not be afraid, for behold, I bring you good news of great JOY; for unto you is born this day in the city of Bethlehem a Savior, who is Christ the Lord." There is great joy in knowing the eternal way. The truth of life for us is found in Jesus the Christ. This is indeed the gospel!

The New Testament is a book of joy. Jesus, our wonderfull teacher, says to us: "These things I have spoken to you, that my joy may be in you, and that your joy may be full" (Jn 15:11). It is only in our joy that we are witnesses for the good news of Jesus. Psalm 98 declares: "Make a joyful noise to the Lord, all the earth;...let the floods clap their hands; let the hills sing for joy together before the Lord" (vv. 4, 8).

Joy comes to us from the presence of the Holy Spirit in our lives. Paul, writing to the Romans, says: "[T]he kingdom of God is not food and drink but righteousness and peace and joy in the Holy Spirit" (14:17).

One of the outstanding thinking persons of our time has been C. S. Lewis. His contribution to the Christian faith is beyond measure, but Lewis started out as an atheist, later moved to being a theist, and then, finally, to being a Christian. He calls his autobiography, *Surprised by Joy.* In it he says: "It never occurred to me that there was any connection between God and joy. I had hoped that the heart of reality might be of just such a kind that we could symbolize it as a place; indeed, I found it to be a Person."

When we know the Holy Spirit, joy can come to us in the face of our own frailties, even when we feel we are without talent. Matthew tells of the unspeakable joy in the hearts of the women who ran to tell the disciples that the Lord had risen (Mt 28:8). Picture yourself present that first Easter, standing before the empty tomb, and feel the great joy of knowing that Jesus has risen.

The presence of the Holy Spirit in a human life is pure joy. Paul put it this way: "We rejoice in our sufferings, knowing that suffering produces endurance, and endurance produces character, and character produces hope; because God's love is poured into our hearts through the Holy Spirit, given to us." This is true joy!

Picture the angel at the door of the empty tomb saying, "I sang at Jesus' birth! I told you at the beginning of Jesus' life that I brought good news of great joy for all people....Well, here it is! It is better than any human could have dreamed. Right?"

PRAYER

O Lord God, we would be children of joy. We would be witnesses of thy Holy Spirit within us. Help us to share with people who seem to have little or no joy. Deepen our faith in Jesus the Christ, so that as we live and love and sacrifice for him, we shall still be surprised by joy. Amen.

FRUIT OF THE SPIRIT—PEACE

Isaiah 9:2-7   John 14:25-27
Ephesians 2:13-18   Colossians 3:12-15

The presence of the Holy Spirit of God in a human life is the essence of peace. The fruits of the Spirit are love... peace. It is not something that we human beings create ourselves. The peace of God passes all our understanding.

Peace is an ingredient of life that most people yearn for but few fully realize. In growing numbers, there are those who seem to believe that they can solve their problems by some means of violence or retaliation. Children carry guns to school for "protection"; people rob and kill to secure money for drugs and alcohol; now there is "road rage." Some minorities use violence in their attempt to obtain justice, believing this a necessary ingredient to achieve peace.

Longfellow once mused: "There is no peace on earth, for hate is strong and mocks the song of peace on earth, goodwill to men." Jeremiah the prophet tells of people who, from the least to the greatest, are greedy for unjust gains and deal falsely: they cry, "Peace! Peace!" when there is no peace.

Isaiah, in the midst of our human inability to create peace, declares that there will be a Messiah: a child will be born who will be called "the Prince of peace." There will be a "peaceable kingdom," and a little child will lead us.

Jesus, this Prince of peace, talks about "My peace." Jesus came to bring repentance and salvation to our souls. To know peace, it is necessary to repent of our alienation from one another and to forgive one another as Christ has forgiven us. St. Paul, speaking to separated peoples says, "[H]e is our peace, who has made us both one, and has broken down the dividing wall of hostility...we both have access in one Spirit to the Father (Eph 2:14,18)." Paul calls God "the God of peace."

Jesus declares, "In the world you have tribulation; but be of good cheer, for I have overcome the world." It is through our faith in Jesus as the Christ, who overcomes the peaceless world, that the Holy Spirit comes into our lives. Jesus' promise is that when the Holy Spirit comes, we will have peace. We are to let the peace of Christ rule in our hearts.

Peace is more than the absence of violence in the world: it is the absence of violence within ourselves. The word, "shalom," we usually translate, "peace," but it means more than peace: it means wholeness and integrity within a human life, and, therefore, peace. The fruit of the integrating Spirit is peace.

PRAYER

Dear Lord God, we come to worship and praise you, for we know that your Holy Spirit presence within us is, indeed, our longed-for peace. We know that Christ is the Prince of peace, who offers us forgiveness, who breaks down the wall of hostility between ourselves and others. We thank you, O God, whose Spirit is Peace. Amen.

FRUIT OF THE SPIRIT—KINDNESS

1 Corinthians 13:4–7   Titus 3:3–7
Ephesians 4:30–32   Galatians 5:22–23

In a book entitled, *Random Acts of Kindness,* the author states that it all began when some one in a restaurant in California wrote on a placemat the words, "Practice random acts of kindness and senseless acts of beauty." Pictures of the saying appeared, then bumper stickers, and from these the book mentioned. Someone said, "The secret of happiness is kindness, seeing others as an extension of one's own self."

The Bible links the source of our kindness to the love of God. We read, "Love (agape) is patient and kind...." Within ourselves we come to realize that kindness is, in reality, the love of God in action. Titus tells us, "We were once foolish, disobedient, led astray,...but when the goodness and loving kindness of God our Savior appeared,...[there was] renewal in the Holy Spirit." Indeed, our Galatians text tells us that the fruit of the Spirit is "...love...kindness."

Kindness in us is the witness we give of God's prevenient grace. The Greek word usually translated, "kindness," is the word used when Jesus related to the sinning woman who anointed his feet.

In our Boy Scout life we were called upon to do at least one good deed per day, because "a scout is trustworthy...kind." Kindness is a graceful deed done without the other person's having to request it.

Kindness may inconvenience us. It is more than pretending to be concerned about someone's condition. It means becoming involved with the personal sorrows and even the pain of other lives to the extent that it may well cost us real sorrow and effort.

Kahlil Gibran declares: "Tenderness and kindness are not signs of weakness and despair but manifestations of strength and resolution." Kindness is the spirit in which we are to live. Our lives are never full and abundant until the spirit of kindness is our ordinary way of living.

Paul, writing to the Ephesians, declares: "[D]o not grieve the Holy Spirit of God, in whom you were sealed for the day of redemption...and be kind to one another, tenderhearted, forgiving one another, as God in Christ forgave you" (4:30–32).

Kindness is God's redemptive Spirit at work. Many years ago, Harry Emerson Fosdick once said, "Redemption takes place when a person who does not have to do it, for the sake of someone who does not deserve it, sacrifices something of his own well-being in behalf of the other." The saving power of God is kindness (grace). The good person is the kind person. Kindness is a lovely quality, because kindness means treating others the way God treats us.

PRAYER

Dear Lord God, we bow before you. We pray that your Holy Spirit will be present within us as kindness. We ask you to touch our lives, to remove our selfishness and to make us whole. Your presence is our spiritual strength. Forgive us, O God, for our lethargy and set us afire with your Holy Spirit so that we may, indeed, be kind to one another. We pray in the name of Jesus, our Savior, who is gracefully kind to us. Amen.

FRUIT OF THE SPIRIT—SELF-CONTROL

Romans 7:15–19; 7:21–8:4

One of the most difficult things for most of us is to confront the reality that is one's self. In so much of our life we seem to be motivated by a spirit inherent within ourselves that we do not like. Without thinking about it, certainly without deciding about it, in some situations, do you not find your subconscious mind bringing forth thoughts or motivating actions unacceptable to you? Many times I find myself acting out of fear, resentment, anger, spite or even revenge, without ever deciding to do so.

A university psychologist set forth a theory called "cognitive dissonance." By this he means a person's awareness of the big gap between ideals and action: between what one holds as moral principles and how one behaves, between goals and deeds.

Paul tells us: "I do not understand my own actions...I can will what is right, but I cannot do it. I do not do the good I want, but the evil I do not want is what I do" (Rom 7:15, 18–19).

In daily living we tend to excuse our ungodly spirit and deeds by saying, "After all, we are only human, what more can you expect?" Our problem is that God does expect more from us and does not accept that which we so commonly excuse. We are forced to confront the truth that the consequences of our spiritual sin is spiritual death. Even though we may want to, in our uncontrolled selves we are spiritually too weak to change. God's Holy Spirit is the only power able to deliver self-control to our inner being.

Jesus comes to baptize us with the Holy Spirit of God that we may have life and have it full and abundant. Faith in Christ opens the door of our hearts enabling the Holy Spirit to take over. Paul declares, "Wretched man that I am! Who will deliver me from this body of death? Thanks be to God through Jesus Christ our Lord...[T]he Spirit of life in Christ Jesus has set me free" (Rom 7:24–25; 8:2).

Self-control is a fruit of God's Holy Spirit presence within. Salvation comes when the grace of God, the Spirit of God at work within, takes charge of our hearts and sets us free from sinful ugliness to become free, beautiful selves in Christ Jesus. This is what the saviorhood of Christ really means.

PRAYER

Dear Holy Spirit God, when we are out of control, we are unhappy, fearful, resentful, ugly creatures. Help us to give the control of our spirits to your Holy Spirit. We long to be the kind of persons we can become only in you. We believe that you have created us to be Spirit-centered, far more loving, far more joyful, far more peaceful than we could ever become on our own. Help us so to surrender to you so that we are totally controlled by you and enjoy the fruit of your Spirit within us, even self-control. Amen.

LISTEN! THE SPIRIT SPEAKS TO THE CHURCHES!

Revelation 2 and 3

The fellowship of believers, the church, in many ways, relates to God as an individual. Its very life is the presence of the Spirit of God, the risen Christ: it is this presence alone who provides the dynamic and the meaning. Indeed, the dynamic is the meaning. The church, as well as the individual, finds its place in history with its witness to the life of the Holy Spirit of God for that particular generation or locality. The Spirit alone builds the church and molds the sacred human life.

The church, or the individual, can become indifferent or callous toward the Spirit and, therefore, self-centered. People, who *are* the church, can come to worship the various "golden calves" present in society. Seekers often declare that the people of the church are too concerned about their organization or prestige in the community.

John of Patmos, in the Book of Revelation, says that while he was "in the Spirit on the Lord's day," (Rev 1:10) messages came to him for the churches of Asia Minor.

His cry to each church was: "Listen to what the Spirit says to the churches."

The Spirit acknowledged their persecutions and, therefore, their suffering. Satan was trying to take their life away from them. They would need to repent of their alienation from the Spirit of God. If they would be faithful and overcome this evil, it would be granted to them to eat of "the tree of life" (the tree forbidden to Adam and Eve). They would be given the crown of life. They would not be subject to the second death, and their names would be inscribed in "the book of life."

As we enter the twenty-first century, many ingredients will be strangely different. We will receive our information from global-wide sources. Our neighbors will be people from across the world who have views and convictions similar to ours. Strangers near and far will live and fight for values different from our own. Churches will be smaller, but of supreme value to us as sources of our faith fellowship and spiritual strength. The presence of the Spirit will be our dynamic, our meaning and our only believable witness.

When Billy Graham received his medal of honor in Washington, he said, "No other century has been so ravaged by such devastating wars, genocide, and tyranny. Terms like 'ethnic cleansing,' 'random violence,' and 'suicide bombing' have become part of our daily vocabulary. As we face a new millennium, I believe that America has gone a long way down the wrong road. If we ever needed God's Spirit, it is now! If we ever needed spiritual renewal, it is now!"

God's Holy Spirit is real and present with us. More than ever, we need to listen to what the Spirit is saying to each of us and to the churches.

PRAYER

Be quiet. Listen for at least a half hour to the Spirit of God.

HOLY SPIRIT—INNER LIGHT

John 1:1–13   Isaiah 30:15   1 John 1:5–7

When William Penn, the Quaker, came, he brought with him a quietness and a worship that was mostly silence. They would call his city, "the city of brotherly love," and the surrounding area, "Penn's Woods." The Quakers, or "Friends," as some are called, have a concept of an "inner light" which comes during a period of silence while "listening" to the Holy Spirit of God. This "silent listening" cannot be separated from their remarkable record of community service and worldwide commitment to work for peace.

Jesus declared: "I am the Light of the world" (Jn 8:12). In the prologue of John we read: "In him was life, and the life was the light of [all people]. The light shines in the darkness, and the darkness has not overcome it" (Jn 1:4–5). The light that was in Jesus is the inner redeeming Spirit of God. Our prayer comes from the Christmas carol by John H. Hopkins, Jr.:

Star of wonder, star of night,
star of royal beauty bright,
westward leading still proceeding,
guide us to thy perfect light.

There is a story of a non-Quaker, who wandered into a Quaker worship time. There was only silence. The man sat down to participate. After about twenty minutes of quiet, the man said to a Friend near by, "When does the service begin?" The Friend responded, "Right after the worship." In listening to the Holy Spirit, we receive a guiding light for our living.

Many of us seem afraid of silence. We want a TV or a "boom box" to be blaring all around us, apparently to override our need to be silent. We often have "soul anxieties" that seem to need noise.

The Psalmist says, "Be still and know that I am God." Adapted from the liturgy of St. James in the fourth century, we sing:

Let all mortal flesh keep silence...
for with blessing in his hand,
Christ our God to earth descended,
our full homage to demand.

Mary Chapin-Carpenter, Grammy Award-winning singer, wrote a song entitled: "Ideas Fall All Around Us Like Stars." An interviewer asked her, "How do you have to be for ideas to fall all around you like the stars?" She replied that it happens in "silence, quiet, solitude." "For God alone my soul waits in silence; from him comes my salvation" (Ps 62:1).

Silence allows the Holy Spirit to break through the barriers erected to keep God out. It gives us unexpected spiritual insights of how we might serve human need around us. Evelyn Underhill declares: "A person of prayer is one who is entirely guided by the Creative Spirit in his or her prayers and work. We, who are finite and constantly changing, need desperately to listen to the One who is changeless." St. John of the Cross said: "The Father has spoken one word from all eternity; and he spoke it in silence. It is in silence that we hear it."

The most poignant and profound teaching of spiritual truth is Jesus' Sermon on the Mount. You and I will never appropriate this spirit-life and these blessings unless we take the time to be silent and allow the Holy Spirit of God to share with us their inner meaning. For Jesus, "the Beyond" was always within.

A pastor's central problem is that his parish family is always demanding that he keep talking about important things and preaching Sunday after Sunday. How desperately the pastor, as well as all of us, needs to take long periods of silent worship just to experience the inner light.

PRAYER

Lord, I know that in the silence of my heart you will speak to me and show me your light. Give me that silence. Let me grow into that silence when I can be one with you. Amen.

—Henri Nouwen

THE SPIRIT OF LIFE

Romans 8:1–11   John 10:7–10   John 6:63

Many people fear that they may live to the end of their days and never know what it means to become fully alive.

We seem to realize there is a profound difference between being an individual born of physical parents, to live a purely physical life, and one who knows the "Spirit of life." We long to know what Jesus meant by "the full and abundant life." "In him was life." Jesus says to us: "It is the spirit that gives life."

The Holy Spirit of God, the Spirit of life, is not just a pleasant attitude, but a healing, life-giving reality a person can experience and know within his or her human life.

Earl Marlotte, once dean of the Boston University School of Theology, wrote a hymn entitled, "Spirit of Life in This New Dawn":

Spirit of Life in this new dawn,
Give us the grace that follows on,
Letting thine all-pervading power
Fulfill the dream of this high hour.

Spirit Creative, give us life,
Lifting the raveled mists of night;
Touch Thou our dust with Spirit-hand,
And make us souls that understand.

The Spirit we perceive in Jesus is indeed the Holy Spirit of the eternal God. "God gave us eternal life, and this life is in his Son" (1 Jn 5:11). When we come to entrust our living to the redeeming Spirit of God in Jesus the Christ, we are born again in the Spirit of God. The Spirit of God in our lives is "the Spirit of life."

Earl Marlotte in his hymn speaks of "the Spirit of Life," but also identifies this with "the Spirit creative," "the Spirit redeeming," "the Spirit consoling" and "the Spirit of love." Is it not the Spirit of life within us that is creative, enabling us to be consoling to others, helping us to redeem society and, in a real way, our witness to God's love?

In our Scripture meditation, Paul uses the word, "flesh" *(sarka),* by which he means human nature or the practice of looking at life and things from a godless point of view. The word "flesh," to Paul applies not just to the physical, but to the spiritual as well. Barclay, in his commentary on Romans, says: "It is this kind of focus in a human being that leads one to spiritual death, a kind of spiritual suicide" *(Book of Romans* [Daily Study Bible Series], Philadelphia: Westminster Press, 1975).

The Spirit of life sets us free from the law of sin and, therefore, of death. "In him was life, and this life was the light of all who came into the world—To all who receive him and believe in his name, he gives power to become children of God." "I have come that you might have life, and have it abundantly!" (Jn 10:10). The Spirit of life comes when we know the one true God and Jesus Christ whom he has sent.

PRAYER

O Holy Spirit of life, come and abide in us now and always. We pray to know what it means to be fully alive in you. Amen.

LET YOUR LIFE SING SPIRIT SONGS TO THE LORD!

Psalm 95:1, 2   Ephesians 5:18b–20
Isaiah 12:5, 6   Psalm 149:1–4
Colossians 3:16

Paul writes to the Ephesians, "[B]e filled with the Spirit, addressing one another in psalms and hymns and spiritual songs, singing and making melody to the Lord with all your heart, always and for everything" (5:18b–20).

All through the Bible people are called upon to sing to the Lord because of their salvation. In the book of Revelation, when one hundred and forty-four thousand who have the name of God on their foreheads stand before the throne of God, they sing a new song to the Lord.

Paul and Silas, on their missionary journey, are jailed in Philippi. They were put in the "inner" jail with their feet in stocks. Still, at midnight, they began to pray and sing hymns to God while the other prisoners listened to them.

Isaiah declares: "Sing to the Lord a new song, his praise from the end of the earth....Let them give glory to the Lord and declare his praise" (42:10).

Historians debate at long length whether, in the early Methodist societies, more people were won to Christ by the preaching of John Wesley or by the hymns of Charles Wesley. Charles Wesley wrote over six thousand hymns. Think of the contribution made to Christian life by such hymns as: "Love Divine, All Loves Excelling"; "Jesus, Lover of My Soul"; "O for a Thousand Tongues to Sing"; "A Charge to Keep I Have."

There is a real difference in the way Roland Hayes or Jesse Norman sings "Were You There When They Crucified My Lord?" and the way most congregations sing it. A singing congregation will sing Earl Marlotte's "Are Ye Able, said The Master"—especially when they come to the chorus, "Lord, we are able!"—in a vastly different way from a listless congregation. Congregations sing with joy and enthusiasm when they feel that God is present in their midst. A spirit song comes from the voice and the heart of a person with the Spirit.

Congregations are empowered when they sing with the Spirit. Paul says, "I will sing with my mind, and I will sing with the Spirit." People can sing with their minds; but it is singing with the Spirit that transforms their lives.

Fanny Crosby has written a hymn:

> To God be the glory, great things he has done;
> so loved he the world that he gave us his Son;
> who yielded his life an atonement for sin;
> and opened the life-gate that all may go in.
> Praise the Lord, praise the Lord,

let the earth hear his voice!
Praise the Lord, praise the Lord;
let the people rejoice! O come to the Father,
   through Jesus the son,
and give him the glory, great things he has
   done.

When people experience the salvation of their souls, they sing with their minds and they sing with the Spirit.

PRAYER

Breathe on me, Breath of God, until I am wholly thine; until all this earthly part of me glows with thy fire divine. Amen.

—Edwin Hatch, inspired by John 20:22

SPIRIT-LED CHILDREN OF GOD

Romans 8:11–17, 24, 37–39

"For all who are led by the Spirit of God are [children] of God....[I]t is the Spirit [of God] bearing witness with our spirit that we are children of God" (Rom 8:14, 16).

Is it not so that one of the major reasons we do not follow Jesus more closely is that we are afraid we might be hurt if we do? If we love our enemies, will they not turn on us and destroy us? If we go the second mile, no one will let us stop there. If we feed the hungry, will we have enough for our own children? If we tithe our incomes, will we be able to pay our bills? If we live for Jesus, will we not die early? In the Spirit, we have no bondage to fear; rather, we have the Spirit of adoption, whereby we cry out to God, "Abba, Spirit."

Our Scripture is telling us that as we allow the Spirit of God to lead us, we become victorious. We find our strength is adequate to our needs, and we find peace and joy in our living. The Spirit sets us free from our bondage to false gods. Isn't it our service to secular and material gods that makes us insecure and afraid? It is when we compromise with our principles to appease people that we become frail and shallow. It is as our spirits identify with the Spirit of God that we realize we belong to God.

In our self-centered or material dependencies, we become afraid of becoming ill or of dying. When, in our faith, we depend on the Spirit of God to lead and sustain us, we become spiritually strong and vital. We feel ourselves heirs of God and joint heirs with Christ.

Without faith, we are strangers to Christ, alien in many ways from God. Allowing the Spirit to lead us, we feel adopted by God, forgiven and reconciled. It is our faith that "...the Spirit of [the One] who raised Jesus from the dead...will give life to our mortal [beings]...through [the] Spirit [who] dwells in you" (Rom 8:11).

If we are children of God, we then become peacemakers in our families, in society and even in the world. When we give ourselves totally to the Spirit, we come to love God with our total beings. If we suffer with Christ in paying whatever price is exacted from us by being love in the world: then, we reap the spirit of Jesus and overcome any doubts we may have about the validity of Christ's way of life. When we feel called by the purpose of God, we discover that this purpose becomes the ultimate focus and meaning of our lives.

PRAYER

Dear Lord God, we would do your will. Help us to believe. We would live for you. Permeate our beings with your Holy Spirit. Take away our bondage to fear; grant that we may live with spiritual strength

*and courage. Help us to know the love of Christ
that we may love each other as Christ has loved us.
If you will abide in us, we will live with peace and
joy. If your Spirit will lead us we will be your children always. Amen.*

THE PRAYER OF THEOPHILUS

Luke 1:1–4   Acts 1:1–8

I am Theophilus—I am one who loves God. I do not know everything about God, but I care for the God I know a little about. I care enough that someone labeled me, *Theophilus,* "one who loves God."

I first learned about Jesus when Luke wrote to me about Jesus' miraculous birth, his life and teachings, about his crucifixion, and then about his resurrection on that first Easter—oh, how I wish I could have been there! Luke was not there either. He had written down what someone had told him. He must have believed it was true.

Now Luke has written me again, telling about the disciples experiencing the risen Jesus and becoming apostles. It is mainly the story of the disciples, now apostles, now empowered by the Holy Spirit, now believing the risen Jesus is truly the Savior of the world.

This book begins with the risen Jesus telling his disciples

that John baptized with water, but before many days they would be baptized with the Holy Spirit of God. The whole story is about people who were indeed baptized with the Holy Spirit, bearing witness to the presence of the risen Lord in their personal lives. No one can read this beautiful and wonder-full account without realizing Someone here is at work besides mere human beings. Indeed, someone has said this book should be called, "The Acts of the Holy Spirit." The Spirit baptism brought the disciples together in a unique fellowship.

When Jesus was crucified, the bewildered disciples did not know where to turn or what to do. Their baptism in the Holy Spirit enabled them to be committed to a mission they could not, by themselves, have envisioned. Luke wrote to me about what had happened. I, Theophilus, pray that I may have enough faith in Christ so that I, too, may be baptized with the Holy Spirit. Amen.

Jesus told the disciples that they would be his witnesses not only in Jerusalem, not only in Judea and in Samaria, but to the very ends of the earth. I pray that I, too, may become a witness for Christ, that I, too, may be part of this great mission that will never end. I will pour my life into people, and they will touch others, and these others still, until the kingdom of God comes. Amen.

PRAYER

Dear Holy Spirit-God, I am overwhelmed by the resurrection of the Lord. I am so disappointed I was not there personally; but my name, "Theophilus," is right—I do love you. I am not worthy to be called a follower of Jesus, but I long to be. No one is ever worthy, but Lord, I pray that you will accept me and baptize me with thy Holy

Spirit. In the name of Jesus, I pray that I, one who loves you, with other believers, may bear witness to the risen Lord and be a part of the church of Jesus Christ our Lord, now and always. Amen.

CELEBRATING THE EUCHARIST

John 13:1–15   Matthew 26:20–30
1 Corinthians 11:23–26

"The eucharist" is the word used to mean the time when we remember with overwhelming gratitude the Last Supper that Jesus had with his disciples. It was the night before he went to the cross—when Jesus said, "Do this in remembrance of me" (1 Cor 11:24). It is a time when we share bread as a symbol of the broken body of Jesus; a time when we drink of the cup and remember our new covenant with God in Christ's blood. To participate in the eucharist is to share in Christ's love for us. It is a sacrament for us as our lives are touched by the Holy Spirit.

The word, *eucharist* means gratitude or thanksgiving—it is a time when we give thanks for Jesus' redeeming sacrifice on our behalf. We remember that Christ was the heart of the world, and the world killed him. It is a time when we remember that it is our sin that crucifies the Lord of life.

It was said about that night in the upper room, "There never was another night like this night..."—the moments of joy the disciples had with the Lord of life the night before he went to the cross to pay the cost of being the love and joy and mercy of God in the world. Doesn't it seem odd to you that Jesus might have been overflowing with joy? We are told, "[It was] for the joy that was set before him [that Jesus] endured the cross..." (Heb 12:2). I wonder if that night the hungry disciples realized the kingdom of God was not the Passover food and drink, but, rather, the righteousness, joy and peace they received from the Spirit in Jesus.

The disciples were humbled as the Lord of life washed their feet, and they heard the command to wash one another's feet. The Spirit of Jesus bestows upon a human life a sacred humility. Being for each other in the Holy Spirit what Jesus has been for us is one way to know companionship with Jesus. We come to the Lord's table to receive spirit and courage for our Christian life. As John Killinger has put it: "Bread for the wilderness; wine for the journey." We need the "Beyond" within our souls to be Christ's people.

Jesus took bread and broke it, saying, "This is my body, which is for you" (1 Cor 11–24). Then he took the cup and gave thanks, saying, "This cup is the new covenant in my blood" (1 Cor 11:25). We who watch Jesus from a distance, think "What strange love this, to take the cup and to give thanks." We, too, come to the table of our Lord to take the cup and to give thanks.

Reflect on this benediction of eucharist:

> We have seen the Light of the world; we have
> broken the bread and poured out the wine; we
> have received the Holy Spirit. We are thankful.

We would be apostles of Christ, witnesses of the Holy Spirit. We must go forth now in his glorious name and live for Christ.

PRAYER

O Lord Christ, O Holy Spirit of God, help us to be life-full witnesses for you. Be with us as we go forth in your name to share with others your Spirit, your love, your cup. Amen.

WALKING IN THE SPIRIT

Galatians 5:16–25   1 Corinthians 13:4–8a
Ephesians 5:8–14   Psalm 101:1–3a

Because God is Love, we are to walk sustained by the Spirit who is love. Because God is light, we are to shun the darkness of immorality, and walk by the Spirit who is light for us. We are to walk with integrity of heart and not set before our eyes anything that is base.

Many times I feel deeply moved by the light and love of God for me and for the people around me. Sometimes I feel that God's love is so evident, that I believe Jesus was sent to me personally. I feel profoundly moved and inspired. As I attempt to walk by the Spirit I realize Jesus is, for me, as well as for others, *the* way and *the* truth and *the* life.

Even though I experience the love of God for me, I am just not sure what the scope of that love is, or what it means. I wonder if you have ever felt this way. This spiritual experience is more than just a feeling; it is a real presence. I want to walk in fellowship with this Holy

Spirit. Our hearts are given to us that we may love with our total beings the God who fellowships with us.

In 1 Corinthians 13:4–8a we are told that Love is patient and kind, that it is not jealous or boastful; it is not arrogant or rude. Love does not insist on its own way; it is not irritable or resentful; it does not rejoice at wrong; it rejoices in the right. Love bears all things, believes all things, hopes all things, endures all things; and it never ends.

Do you suppose that God's love in Christ is that kind of love? Can you believe that God in his relationship to you and me is patient and kind: that God on our behalf bears all things, believes in us, hopes in us, endures all things for us—that God never stops loving us?—that we shall walk by the Spirit of God who is light and love forever?

When we walk in the Spirit the fruit of the Spirit within us is love and joy, and peace. We are to walk "in love" as we see the love of God revealed to us in Jesus the Christ. The psalmist declares, "I will walk with integrity of heart" (101:2). We sing the words of Washington Gladden, "O Master, let me walk with thee in lowly paths of service free." In the Holy Spirit, the command is not only to "talk the talk, but to walk the walk."

What does the Bible mean that we are to love ourselves? Does it mean when we walk in the Spirit, we are to be patient with ourselves, hope in ourselves, believe in ourselves and never to give up? Experiencing "the Beyond" within our lives, enables us to have faith in ourselves, the needed self-esteem for a confident and significant life.

What does it mean that I should love you and even my enemies as I love myself? Is to walk in the Spirit for me to be patient and kind toward you, not to insist on my own way; and to believe in you?—even to hope and to believe in my enemies, realizing that they are not God's enemies? "We are to walk in light as children of light."

To walk in the Spirit is to meditate on the God who is love with all my heart and mind and soul and strength, and to love you as God in Christ loves me. Is not our need to know what God has in mind for us? To walk in the Spirit is to entrust our lives to the Christ who is the way and the truth of God and the sacred life in our midst. To walk in the Spirit is the sacred life for us.

PRAYER

Lord God in Christ, help us to meditate on the Spirit of Christ that he may become for us the way and the truth and the life. Help me to walk in thy Spirit and to experience within myself the fruit of thy Spirit. Help me to walk in the Spirit with appreciation of my own life and in the realization of how sacred are the lives of my neighbors and even my enemies. Help me to know that you love your whole creation and care personally for me. In this precious moment of devotion I pray with praise and eternal gratefulness that I may walk each day in thy Spirit. Amen.